MATHEMATICS
Skills, Concepts, Problem Solving

Illustrations: Page 12 (boys): Margaret Lindmark; Page 20 (soda cans): www.shutterstock.com, Dic Liew; Page 26: John Norton; Pages 53, 74 (rat), 84 (cooking, winter), 88 (scale): Laurie Conley; Pages 62, 85: Marty Husted; Page 65: Jane Yamada; Page 84 (beach, stove); Matt LeBarre

Photo Credits: Front Cover: Corbis/Punchstock; Page 3: www.shutterstock.com, David Lee; Pages 17, 42 (top): www.shutterstock.com, Elena Elisseeva; Page 19: www.istockphoto.com/stray_cat; Page 22: www.shutterstock.com, Alon Othnay; Page 25: www.shutterstock.com, STILLFX; Page 28: www.shutterstock.com, Stephen Coburn; Page 32 (top): www.shutterstock.com, Vlises Sepúlveda Déniz; (bottom): www.shutterstock.com, dpwebphotos; Page 36: www.shutterstock.com, ilker canikligil; Page 39: www.shutterstock.com, Petros Tsonis; Pages 42 (bottom), 67 (bottom), 73 (top): www.shutterstock.com, Morgan Lane Photography; Page 52: www.shutterstock.com, Serg Zastavkin; Page 54 (top): www.istockphoto.com/Dervical; (bottom): www.photos.com; Page 61 (top): www.shutterstock.com, Paul Yates; (bottom): www.shutterstock.com, Lynn Watson; Page 64: www.shutterstock.com, goran cakmazovic; Page 67 (top): www.photos.com; Page 69: www.shutterstock.com, Dole; Page 73 (bottom): www.shutterstock.com, Monkey Business Images; Page 77 (top): www.shutterstock.com, Laitr Keiows; (bottom): www.shutterstock.com, Joe Gough; Page 87: www.shutterstock.com, Bob Ainsworth; Page 91: www.shutterstock.com, Jaren Jai Wicklund

ISBN 978-0-8454-5861-7

Copyright © 2009 The Continental Press, Inc.

Continental

Contents

3 ..... Place Value: Through Hundred Thousands
4 ..... Comparing and Ordering Numbers
5 ..... Rounding Numbers
6 ..... Place Value: Millions and Billions
7 ..... Addition and Subtraction: Basic Facts
8 ..... Properties of Addition
9 ..... Problem Solving: Choosing the Operation
10 ..... Adding Two- and Three-Digit Numbers
11 ..... Adding Larger Numbers
12 ..... Subtracting Two-Digit Numbers
13 ..... Subtracting Three-Digit Numbers
14 ..... Subtracting Across Zeros
15 ..... Subtracting Larger Numbers
16 ..... Estimating Sums and Differences
17 ..... Problem Solving: Using Estimation
18 ..... Checking Addition and Subtraction
19 ..... Problem Solving: Writing a Number Sentence
20 ..... Multiplication: Basic Facts
21 ..... Properties of Multiplication
22 ..... Problem Solving: Making an Organized List
23 ..... Multiplying Two- and Three-Digit Numbers
24 ..... Multiplying Larger Numbers
25 ..... Problem Solving: Identifying Insufficient Information
26 ..... Division: Basic Facts
27 ..... Division with Remainders
28 ..... Problem Solving: Interpreting a Remainder
29 ..... Dividing Two- and Three-Digit Numbers
30 ..... Dividing Larger Numbers
31 ..... Problem Solving: Identifying Extra Information
32 ..... Problem Solving: Using Multiplication and Division
33 ..... Multiplying by Tens and Hundreds
34 ..... Multiplying by Two-Digit Numbers
35 ..... Multiplying by Three-Digit Numbers
36 ..... Problem Solving: Planning Two-Step Solutions
37 ..... Dividing by Tens
38 ..... Dividing by Two-Digit Numbers: One-Digit Quotients
39 ..... Dividing by Two-Digit Numbers: Two-Digit Quotients
40 ..... Dividing by Two-Digit Numbers: Larger Quotients
41 ..... Estimating Products and Quotients
42 ..... Problem Solving: Using the Four Operations
43 ..... Order of Operations
44 ..... Finding Multiples
45 ..... Finding Factors
46 ..... Prime and Composite Numbers
47 ..... Problem Solving: Guessing and Checking
48 ..... Fractions
49 ..... Equivalent Fractions
50 ..... Simplifying Fractions
51 ..... Adding and Subtracting Fractions with Like Denominators
52 ..... Adding Fractions with Unlike Denominators
53 ..... Subtracting Fractions with Unlike Denominators
54 ..... Problem Solving: Using Fractions
55 ..... Mixed Numbers
56 ..... Changing Mixed Numbers to Fractions
57 ..... Comparing and Ordering Fractions and Mixed Numbers
58 ..... Adding and Subtracting Mixed Numbers with Like Denominators
59 ..... Adding Mixed Numbers with Unlike Denominators
60 ..... Subtracting Mixed Numbers with Unlike Denominators
61 ..... Problem Solving: Using Mixed Numbers

62 ..... Adding and Subtracting Fractions and Mixed Numbers—Practice
63 ..... Multiplying Fractions
64 ..... Multiplying Fractions and Whole Numbers
65 ..... Multiplying Fractions and Mixed Numbers
66 ..... Dividing Whole Numbers by Fractions
67 ..... Problem Solving: Using the Four Operations with Fractions
68 ..... Decimals: Place Value
69 ..... Comparing and Ordering Decimals
70 ..... Adding Decimals
71 ..... Subtracting Decimals
72 ..... Adding and Subtracting Decimals
73 ..... Problem Solving: Adding and Subtracting Decimals
74 ..... Multiplying Decimals
75 ..... Multiplying and Dividing Decimals by 10; 100; 1,000
76 ..... Dividing Decimals
77 ..... Problem Solving: Using the Four Operations with Decimals
78 ..... Problem Solving: Using Units of Time
79 ..... Problem Solving: Finding Elapsed Time
80 ..... Problem Solving: Using a Schedule
81 ..... Measurement: Millimeter and Centimeter
82 ..... Measurement: Meter and Kilometer
83 ..... Measurement: Metric Units of Capacity and Mass
84 ..... Measurement: Degrees Celsius
85 ..... Problem Solving: Using Hidden Information
86 ..... Measurement: Fractions of an Inch
87 ..... Measurement: Customary Units of Length
88 ..... Measurement: Customary Units of Capacity and Weight
89 ..... Problem Solving: Using a Recipe
90 ..... Problem Solving: Making a Table
91 ..... Ratios
92 ..... Equal Ratios
93 ..... Problem Solving: Using a Scale Drawing
94 ..... Introduction to Percent
95 ..... Finding a Percent of a Number
96 ..... Finding a Percent
97 ..... Problem Solving: Using Percents
98 ..... Geometry: Basic Concepts
99 ..... Geometry: Angles
100 ..... Geometry: Measuring Angles
101 ..... Geometry: Parallel and Intersecting Lines
102 ..... Geometry: Triangles
103 ..... Geometry: Quadrilaterals
104 ..... Geometry: Congruent and Similar Polygons
105 ..... Geometry: Symmetry
106 ..... Geometry: Circles
107 ..... Geometry: Perimeter
108 ..... Geometry: Area
109 ..... Geometry: Area of Triangles
110 ..... Geometry: Solid Figures
111 ..... Geometry: Volume
112 ..... Problem Solving: Drawing a Picture
113 ..... Geometry: Ordered Pairs
114 ..... Reading and Making Bar Graphs
115 ..... Reading and Making Line Graphs
116 ..... Mean, Median, Range
117 ..... Problem Solving: Using a Circle Graph
118 ..... Problem Solving: Making a Tree Diagram
119 ..... Probability
120 ..... More Probability

This stadium holds one hundred two thousand, seven hundred twenty-one (102,721) people.

Write each number in standard form.

1. fifty-two _____
2. six hundred three _____
3. one hundred fifteen _____
4. nine hundred ninety _____
5. forty-three thousand, one hundred seventy-seven _____
6. nine thousand, eight hundred thirty-four _____
7. seven hundred twenty thousand, four hundred eleven _____
8. two hundred sixty-one thousand, three hundred ninety-eight _____

Write each number in expanded form.

9. 109,075 = _____ 100,000 + 9,000 + 70 + 5 _____
10. 5,408 = _____
11. 46,300 = _____
12. 30,864 = _____
13. 624,009 = _____
14. 405,068 = _____

Write the total value of the underlined digit.

15. <u>3</u>,540 _____ 3,000 _____
16. <u>8</u>0,619 _____
17. <u>9</u>00,005 _____
18. 7<u>2</u>,824 _____
19. 210,<u>7</u>52 _____
20. 5<u>5</u>3,400 _____

21. 6,<u>0</u>20 _____
22. <u>3</u>00,085 _____
23. 2<u>9</u>,694 _____
24. 8,4<u>2</u>1 _____
25. <u>6</u>5,858 _____
26. <u>7</u>92,062 _____

The symbol > means *is greater than*. The symbol < means *is less than*.

$$63 > 62 \qquad 4,587 < 4,857$$

Notice that the symbol always points toward the smaller number.

Write > or < in each circle.

1. 56 ◯ 65

2. 2,109 ◯ 2,108

3. 49,798 ◯ 49,806

4. 734 ◯ 729

5. 4,284 ◯ 4,264

6. 32,495 ◯ 214,210

7. 409 ◯ 490

8. 9,884 ◯ 9,798

9. 950,301 ◯ 950,288

10. 8,706 ◯ 8,670

11. 10,370 ◯ 1,470

12. 814,000 ◯ 804,956

Below is a table showing the highest mountain on each continent. Write number sentences to compare the heights of the mountains for each pair of continents.

Continent	Mountain	Height in Feet
Africa	Kilimanjaro	19,340
Antarctica	Vinson	16,066
Asia	Everest	29,035
Australia	Kosciusko	7,310
Europe	Elbrus	18,510
North America	McKinley	20,320
South America	Aconcagua	22,834

13. Asia / South America

_____ ◯ _____

14. Australia / Antarctica

_____ ◯ _____

15. Europe / Africa

_____ ◯ _____

16. South America / North America

_____ ◯ _____

List the names of the mountains in order from highest to lowest.

_____

_____

_____

_____

_____

_____

_____

Comparing and Ordering Numbers

Round to the nearest **ten** by looking at the **ones**: 5<u>8</u> → 60
Round to the nearest **hundred** by looking at the **tens**: 2<u>1</u>9 → 200
Round to the nearest **thousand** by looking at the **hundreds**: 3,<u>5</u>12 → 4,000

Remember these rules:
  If the digit you are looking at is 4 or less, round down.
  If the digit you are looking at is 5 or more, round up.

Round each number to the nearest—

ten	hundred	thousand
1. 47 _____	9. 123 _____	17. 8,499 _____
2. 85 _____	10. 515 _____	18. 3,543 _____
3. 21 _____	11. 872 _____	19. 2,006 _____
4. 52 _____	12. 349 _____	20. 6,821 _____
5. 109 _____	13. 650 _____	21. 15,681 _____
6. 682 _____	14. 1,097 _____	22. 91,218 _____
7. 316 _____	15. 4,647 _____	23. 41,903 _____
8. 934 _____	16. 2,833 _____	24. 83,529 _____

Below is a list of distances between major cities. Round each distance to the nearest ten, hundred, and thousand.

	Miles	Tens	Hundreds	Thousands
25. Miami to New York	1,331	_____	_____	_____
26. Chicago to Los Angeles	2,095	_____	_____	_____
27. Boston to Cincinnati	876	_____	_____	_____
28. Denver to Philadelphia	1,770	_____	_____	_____
29. New Orleans to Seattle	2,612	_____	_____	_____
30. Minneapolis to Phoenix	1,644	_____	_____	_____
31. Las Vegas to Detroit	2,015	_____	_____	_____

The population of Earth is six billion, seven hundred thirty-six million (6,736,000,000).

Write each number in standard form.

1. three billion, five hundred thousand _____

2. seventy-eight million, one hundred nineteen _____

3. fifty-four billion, eighteen million, fifty _____

4. nine-hundred eighty-one billion _____

5. four hundred million, twenty-six thousand _____

6. twenty billion, one million, ninety-two thousand _____

Write the total value of the underlined digit.

7. 3,0<u>9</u>2,011,217 _____

8. 7<u>2</u>,903,629,000 _____

9. <u>1</u>41,893,742 _____

10. <u>4</u>26,008,091,012 _____

11. 2<u>5</u>,000,500 _____

12. 9,<u>8</u>66,654 _____

Use the table below to answer the following questions.

Continent	Population
Africa	922,000,000
Asia	3,800,000,000
Australia	30,000,000
Europe	710,000,000
North America	515,000,000
South America	371,000,000

13. Which continent has the smallest population?

_____

14. Which continent has the largest population?

_____

15. Which has more people, North America or

South America? _____

16. Where do fewer people live, in Europe or in

Africa? _____

Addition and subtraction are **inverse,** or opposite, operations.
You can think of addition to help you subtract.

$$\begin{array}{r} 12 \\ -\ 8 \\ \hline 4 \end{array} \qquad \begin{array}{r} 8 \\ +4 \\ \hline 12 \end{array}$$

↑
Difference

Add or subtract. Watch the signs.

1. $\begin{array}{r} 4 \\ +6 \\ \hline \end{array}$ 2. $\begin{array}{r} 15 \\ -\ 8 \\ \hline \end{array}$ 3. $\begin{array}{r} 8 \\ +3 \\ \hline \end{array}$ 4. $\begin{array}{r} 12 \\ -\ 6 \\ \hline \end{array}$ 5. $\begin{array}{r} 5 \\ +9 \\ \hline \end{array}$ 6. $\begin{array}{r} 16 \\ -\ 7 \\ \hline \end{array}$

7. $\begin{array}{r} 12 \\ -\ 5 \\ \hline \end{array}$ 8. $\begin{array}{r} 9 \\ +8 \\ \hline \end{array}$ 9. $\begin{array}{r} 10 \\ -\ 7 \\ \hline \end{array}$ 10. $\begin{array}{r} 9 \\ +9 \\ \hline \end{array}$ 11. $\begin{array}{r} 13 \\ -\ 6 \\ \hline \end{array}$ 12. $\begin{array}{r} 6 \\ +5 \\ \hline \end{array}$

13. $\begin{array}{r} 8 \\ +6 \\ \hline \end{array}$ 14. $\begin{array}{r} 16 \\ -\ 9 \\ \hline \end{array}$ 15. $\begin{array}{r} 8 \\ +4 \\ \hline \end{array}$ 16. $\begin{array}{r} 13 \\ -\ 8 \\ \hline \end{array}$ 17. $\begin{array}{r} 4 \\ +9 \\ \hline \end{array}$ 18. $\begin{array}{r} 15 \\ -\ 6 \\ \hline \end{array}$

19. $\begin{array}{r} 9 \\ +3 \\ \hline \end{array}$ 20. $\begin{array}{r} 7 \\ +7 \\ \hline \end{array}$ 21. $\begin{array}{r} 10 \\ -\ 2 \\ \hline \end{array}$ 22. $\begin{array}{r} 15 \\ -\ 9 \\ \hline \end{array}$ 23. $\begin{array}{r} 8 \\ +8 \\ \hline \end{array}$ 24. $\begin{array}{r} 9 \\ +4 \\ \hline \end{array}$

25. $\begin{array}{r} 15 \\ -\ 7 \\ \hline \end{array}$ 26. $\begin{array}{r} 10 \\ -\ 5 \\ \hline \end{array}$ 27. $\begin{array}{r} 6 \\ +7 \\ \hline \end{array}$ 28. $\begin{array}{r} 7 \\ +4 \\ \hline \end{array}$ 29. $\begin{array}{r} 14 \\ -\ 5 \\ \hline \end{array}$ 30. $\begin{array}{r} 17 \\ -\ 9 \\ \hline \end{array}$

Use the chart to solve each problem.

MILES RUN

Day	Amy	Jim
Mon.	8	8
Tues.	8	14
Wed.	5	7
Thurs.	12	13
Fri.	15	7

31. How many miles did Jim run this week?

32. How many miles did Amy run this week?

33. What is the difference in total miles run?

Addition and Subtraction: Basic Facts

Read each property below. Then solve the problems beside it.

COMMUTATIVE PROPERTY

$$\begin{array}{c} 6 \\ +7 \\ \hline 13 \end{array} > \text{Addends} < \begin{array}{c} 7 \\ +6 \\ \hline 13 \end{array}$$

Sums

If the order of the addends changes, the sum remains the same.

1. $\begin{array}{r} 8 \\ +9 \\ \hline \end{array}$ $\begin{array}{r} 9 \\ +8 \\ \hline \end{array}$ 2. $\begin{array}{r} 5 \\ +8 \\ \hline \end{array}$ $\begin{array}{r} 8 \\ +5 \\ \hline \end{array}$ 3. $\begin{array}{r} 8 \\ +6 \\ \hline \end{array}$ $\begin{array}{r} 6 \\ +8 \\ \hline \end{array}$

4. $\begin{array}{r} 6 \\ +9 \\ \hline \end{array}$ $\begin{array}{r} 9 \\ +6 \\ \hline \end{array}$ 5. $\begin{array}{r} 3 \\ +7 \\ \hline \end{array}$ $\begin{array}{r} 7 \\ +3 \\ \hline \end{array}$ 6. $\begin{array}{r} 9 \\ +7 \\ \hline \end{array}$ $\begin{array}{r} 7 \\ +9 \\ \hline \end{array}$

ZERO PROPERTY

$$\begin{array}{c} 6 \\ +0 \\ \hline 6 \end{array} \qquad \begin{array}{c} 0 \\ +4 \\ \hline 4 \end{array}$$

If one of the addends is 0, the sum is the other addend.

7. $\begin{array}{r} 7 \\ +0 \\ \hline \end{array}$ 8. $\begin{array}{r} 0 \\ +5 \\ \hline \end{array}$ 9. $\begin{array}{r} 3 \\ +0 \\ \hline \end{array}$ 10. $\begin{array}{r} 9 \\ +0 \\ \hline \end{array}$

11. $\begin{array}{r} 0 \\ +8 \\ \hline \end{array}$ 12. $\begin{array}{r} 0 \\ +6 \\ \hline \end{array}$ 13. $\begin{array}{r} 4 \\ +0 \\ \hline \end{array}$ 14. $\begin{array}{r} 1 \\ +0 \\ \hline \end{array}$

ASSOCIATIVE PROPERTY

$$\begin{array}{c} 4 \\ 5 \\ +6 \\ \hline 15 \end{array}\Big)9 \qquad \begin{array}{c} 4 \\ 5 \\ +6 \\ \hline 15 \end{array}\Big)10$$

If the grouping of the addends changes, the sum remains the same.

15. $\begin{array}{r} 3 \\ 7 \\ +5 \\ \hline \end{array}$ 16. $\begin{array}{r} 9 \\ 7 \\ +1 \\ \hline \end{array}$ 17. $\begin{array}{r} 3 \\ 8 \\ +2 \\ \hline \end{array}$ 18. $\begin{array}{r} 3 \\ 3 \\ +7 \\ \hline \end{array}$

19. $9 + 3 + 4 + 2 =$ _____   20. $6 + 9 + 0 + 1 =$ _____

Write the number that makes each number sentence true.

21. $9 + 6 =$ ____ $+ 9$ 22. $5 + 0 + 6 =$ ____ $+ 6$

23. $4 + 2 + 1 =$ ____ $+ 1$ 24. $4 + 3 = 3 +$ ____

25. $0 + 9 =$ ____ $+ 0$ 26. $2 + 7 + 2 =$ ____ $+ 4$

27. $8 + 7 =$ ____ $+ 8$ 28. $6 + 9 + 1 =$ ____ $+ 10$

29. $7 + 7 + 2 = 7 +$ ____   30. $9 + 4 =$ ____ $+ 9$

Properties of Addition

Step 1. Read the problem carefully.
Step 2. Think: What do I know?
                What must I find out?
                What operation should I use?
Step 3. Solve. Write the problem and find the answer.
Step 4. Check the answer. Does it make sense?

Use the four steps above to find answers to these problems.

1. Sergio put 9 gallons of water in his 18-gallon tank. How much more water must he add to fill the tank?

2. Carlota has 7 guppies. She wants to get 8 more. How many guppies will she have then?

3. At the Tropical Tanks Fish Shop, there are 17 neon tetras in a tank. A customer buys 8 of them. How many neon tetras are left in the tank?

4. Edmond has a saltwater tank with 7 shrimp and 5 crabs in it. How many shrimp and crabs does he have in all?

5. Alicia has 2 angelfish, 6 platies, and 8 guppies. How many tropical fish does she have in all?

6. Vladimir has 14 cardinal tetras and 8 neon tetras. How many more cardinal tetras does he have than neon tetras?

7. Megan's goldfish is 3 inches long. Goldfish in ponds sometimes grow 12 inches long. How much longer could Megan's goldfish grow in a pond?

8. A tank holds 5 sea anemones, 3 sponges, and 3 starfish. How many of these creatures does the tank hold in all?

Problem Solving: Choosing the Operation

9

Add. Regroup as often as necessary.

1.
  1
  78
 +86
 ───
 164

2.
  42
 +53

3.
  23
 +67

4.
  17
 +35

5.
  64
 + 6

6.
  16
  12
 +27

7.
  63
  42
 +84

8.
  26
  90
 +29

9.
  21
  37
 +18

10.
  73
  57
 +60

11.
   1 1
 $2.77
 +0.69
 ─────
 $3.46

12.
 $1.86
 +1.35

13.
 $0.75
 +8.25

14.
 $4.61
 +6.42

15.
 $7.39
 +5.29

16.
  755
 + 47

17.
  103
 +308

18.
  567
 +164

19.
  268
 +490

20.
  355
 +336

21.
  415
  103
 +264

22.
  322
  247
 +128

23.
  121
  316
 + 76

24.
  519
   88
 +643

25.
  109
  870
 + 21

Use the map to find the total distance in kilometers between points on the Erie Canal.

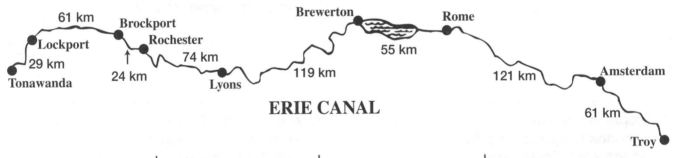

ERIE CANAL

61 km — Lockport — Brockport — Rochester — 74 km — Lyons — 119 km — Brewerton — 55 km — Rome — 121 km — Amsterdam — 61 km — Troy
29 km — Tonawanda; 24 km

26. Tonawanda to Brockport

27. Brockport to Brewerton

28. Brewerton to Troy

29. Tonawanda to Troy

Adding Two- and Three-Digit Numbers

Add. Regroup as often as necessary.

1.
$$1\ 1$$
$$5,308$$
$$+1,764$$
$$\overline{7,072}$$

2.
$$3,488$$
$$+2,196$$

3.
$$1,574$$
$$+6,921$$

4.
$$7,859$$
$$+7,897$$

5.
$$67,207$$
$$+\ 8,499$$

6.
$$18,379$$
$$+25,698$$

7.
$$96,348$$
$$+68,845$$

8.
$$21,544$$
$$+39,976$$

9.
$$40,682$$
$$+470,349$$

10.
$$591,304$$
$$+294,963$$

11.
$$149,338$$
$$+195,872$$

12.
$$238,575$$
$$+181,478$$

13.
$$5,368$$
$$1,208$$
$$+8,143$$

14.
$$21,785$$
$$36,325$$
$$+24,295$$

15.
$$685,294$$
$$73,736$$
$$+101,405$$

16.
$$262,327$$
$$185,307$$
$$+264,396$$

To solve the riddle, find the answers to the problems above in the code box. Then write the matching letters in the correct blanks.

Why did the farmer scold the chickens?

___ ___ ___ ___   ___ ___ ___ ___
10 6   9   3   1   4   9   7

___ ___ ___ ___   ___ ___ ___ ___ ___ ___ ___
11 16 13 8   8   2   5   12 1   2   12 9

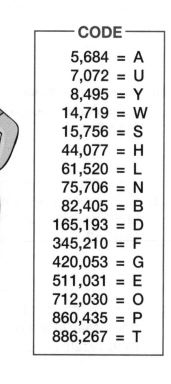

CODE

5,684 = A
7,072 = U
8,495 = Y
14,719 = W
15,756 = S
44,077 = H
61,520 = L
75,706 = N
82,405 = B
165,193 = D
345,210 = F
420,053 = G
511,031 = E
712,030 = O
860,435 = P
886,267 = T

You can't subtract 8 from 2. Regroup 1 ten as 10 ones. Now you have 5 tens and 12 ones. Subtract the ones, and then subtract the tens.

```
  T|O
  5|12
  6|2
 -3|8
  2|4
```

Regroup 1 ten as 10 ones. Now you have 8 tens and 10 ones. Subtract.

```
  T|O
  8|10
  9|0
 -2|7
  6|3
```

Subtract.

1. 86
   −32

2. 80
   −14

3. 47
   −18

4. 91
   −65

5. 65
   − 9

6. 54
   −17

7. 40
   −15

8. 27
   −18

9. 83
   −49

10. 31
    − 7

11. 76
    −28

12. 92
    −16

13. 51
    −45

14. 64
    −12

15. 91
    −33

16. 88
    −19

17. 43
    −20

18. 75
    −57

19. 30
    −13

20. 72
    −37

21. 56
    −35

22. 63
    −14

23. 80
    − 6

24. 91
    −79

25. How much more does Adam weigh than Luke?

_____

26. How much less does Luke weigh than Martin?

_____

27. How much more does Martin weigh than Adam?

Adam

Luke

Martin

45 kilograms

38 kilograms

60 kilograms

Subtracting Two-Digit Numbers

Regroup 1 hundred as 10 tens. Subtract.

H	T	O
5	12	
$\cancel{6}$	$\cancel{2}$	8
−2	4	6
3	8	2

Sometimes you must regroup more than once.

H	T	O
	12	
4	$\cancel{2}$	11
$\cancel{5}$	$\cancel{3}$	$\cancel{1}$
−3	8	6
1	4	5

Subtract.

1.
$$\begin{array}{r} 975 \\ -406 \\ \hline \end{array}$$

2.
$$\begin{array}{r} 528 \\ -344 \\ \hline \end{array}$$

3.
$$\begin{array}{r} 258 \\ -\ 89 \\ \hline \end{array}$$

4.
$$\begin{array}{r} 723 \\ -227 \\ \hline \end{array}$$

5.
$$\begin{array}{r} 461 \\ -175 \\ \hline \end{array}$$

6.
$$\begin{array}{r} 436 \\ -165 \\ \hline \end{array}$$

7.
$$\begin{array}{r} 672 \\ -294 \\ \hline \end{array}$$

8.
$$\begin{array}{r} 941 \\ -283 \\ \hline \end{array}$$

9.
$$\begin{array}{r} 850 \\ -757 \\ \hline \end{array}$$

10.
$$\begin{array}{r} 154 \\ -\ 68 \\ \hline \end{array}$$

11.
$$\begin{array}{r} 346 \\ -147 \\ \hline \end{array}$$

12.
$$\begin{array}{r} 724 \\ -348 \\ \hline \end{array}$$

13.
$$\begin{array}{r} 631 \\ -\ 75 \\ \hline \end{array}$$

14.
$$\begin{array}{r} 586 \\ -479 \\ \hline \end{array}$$

15.
$$\begin{array}{r} 823 \\ -519 \\ \hline \end{array}$$

16.
$$\begin{array}{r} \$7.92 \\ -2.85 \\ \hline \end{array}$$

17.
$$\begin{array}{r} \$6.75 \\ -1.39 \\ \hline \end{array}$$

18.
$$\begin{array}{r} \$9.82 \\ -2.34 \\ \hline \end{array}$$

19.
$$\begin{array}{r} \$5.40 \\ -4.56 \\ \hline \end{array}$$

20.
$$\begin{array}{r} \$8.60 \\ -0.92 \\ \hline \end{array}$$

Find the amount that each item has been reduced.

BEACH SALE!

T-shirts
were $8.50   now $7.99

Beach Towels
were $9.45   now $6.78

Beach Balls
were $3.33   now $1.62

Sand Buckets
were $5.70   now $3.95

21. a T-shirt

22. a beach towel

23. a beach ball

24. a sand bucket

You can't subtract from 0. Take 1 from the next place on the left and regroup it in place of the 0.

H	T	O
	7 10	
8̸	0̸	9
−1	5	3
6	5	6

H	T	O
	9	
3	1̸0̸	10
4̸	0̸	0̸
−	7	2
3	2	8

H	T	O
		10
4	0̸	12
5̸	1̸	2̸
−2	9	6
2	1	6

Subtract.

1. 905
   −476

2. 500
   −341

3. 208
   −189

4. 314
   −228

5. 707
   −539

6. 400
   −155

7. 602
   −394

8. 913
   − 84

9. 800
   −637

10. 116
    − 48

11. 302
    −147

12. 700
    −378

13. 618
    − 75

14. 506
    −479

15. 813
    −595

16. $7.11
    −2.85

17. $3.00
    −0.39

18. $9.00
    −2.74

19. $5.10
    −3.56

20. $8.01
    −1.92

21. Dan bought a book about stars that cost $5.35. He gave the store clerk $6.00. How much change did Dan get?

_____

22. The book lists 205 bright stars in the night sky. Dan can pick out 87 of them. How many stars does he have to find yet?

Subtracting Across Zeros

Subtract. Regroup as often as necessary.

1.
  711
  6,8̶1̶4
 −2,793
 ———
  4,021

2.
  9,352
 −3,613
 ———

3.
  2,503
 −1,840
 ———

4.
  3,310
 − 709
 ———

5.
  4,029
 −1,674
 ———

6.
  5,700
 −1,851
 ———

7.
  8,042
 −3,941
 ———

8.
  7,213
 −5,679
 ———

9.
  78,150
 −68,470
 ———

10.
  31,235
 −15,139
 ———

11.
  50,067
 −21,702
 ———

12.
  46,000
 − 6,399
 ———

13.
  81,309
 −48,737
 ———

14.
  64,072
 −58,200
 ———

15.
  29,980
 −19,895
 ———

16.
  736,014
 − 28,678
 ———

17.
  582,431
 −180,952
 ———

18.
  400,158
 −369,023
 ———

19.
  190,002
 −185,742
 ———

20.
  965,304
 −374,839
 ———

21. Mona bought a DVD of her favorite movie for $24.50. Another store asked $28.25 for it. How much did Mona save?

22. Zhong wants to buy a Blu-ray disc player that costs $259.50. He has only $198.75. How much more does he need?

23. A television was on sale for $545.20. The regular price was $639.99. How much cheaper is it on sale?

24. A laptop computer regularly costs $1,279.99. It is on sale for $899.88. How much less does it cost on sale?

Estimate sums and differences by rounding the numbers to be added or subtracted.

$$\begin{array}{r} \$3.88 \\ +5.19 \\ \hline \end{array}$$

$4.00 plus $5.00 is $9.00.
So the sum is about $9.00

$$\begin{array}{r} 6,975 \\ -1,016 \\ \hline \end{array}$$

7,000 minus 1,000 is 6,000.
So the difference is about 6,000.

Estimate each answer. Then solve each problem and compare answers.

1.
$$\begin{array}{r} 195 \\ +496 \\ \hline \end{array}$$
about _____

2.
$$\begin{array}{r} \$6.84 \\ -2.96 \\ \hline \end{array}$$
about _____

3.
$$\begin{array}{r} \$5.08 \\ +3.79 \\ \hline \end{array}$$
about _____

4.
$$\begin{array}{r} \$32.10 \\ -19.50 \\ \hline \end{array}$$
about _____

5.
$$\begin{array}{r} \$75.25 \\ +24.60 \\ \hline \end{array}$$
about _____

6.
$$\begin{array}{r} 4,052 \\ -\ \ 894 \\ \hline \end{array}$$
about _____

7.
$$\begin{array}{r} 8,120 \\ -5,195 \\ \hline \end{array}$$
about _____

8.
$$\begin{array}{r} 1,792 \\ +9,285 \\ \hline \end{array}$$
about _____

9.
$$\begin{array}{r} \$99.06 \\ -55.18 \\ \hline \end{array}$$
about _____

10.
$$\begin{array}{r} 274 \\ 515 \\ +131 \\ \hline \end{array}$$
about _____

11.
$$\begin{array}{r} 395 \\ 222 \\ +489 \\ \hline \end{array}$$
about _____

12.
$$\begin{array}{r} 107 \\ 316 \\ +293 \\ \hline \end{array}$$
about _____

SKI TRAILS

Lake Trail
2,945 feet

Oaks Trail
6,022 feet

Peak Trail
9,105 feet

13. How much longer is Peak Trail than Lake Trail?

14. How long are Lake Trail and Peak Trail together?

15. How much shorter is Lake Trail than Oaks Trail?

Estimating Sums and Differences

For some problems, an exact answer is not needed.

At the mall, Charlotte can't decide between two dresses. One costs $42.88 and the other, $52.75. Would they cost more than $100.00 together?

First, round the prices.

$42.88 is about $43.
$52.75 is about $53.

Then add.

$43
+53
——
$96

No, together the dresses would not cost more than $100.

Use estimates to find the answer to each question.

1. Aaron has $30.00. He wants to buy a shirt that costs $12.95 and a pair of shorts for $18.99. Does he have enough for both?

2. Jocelyn went to the mall with $25.36. She paid $16.88 for a belt. About how much did she have left?

3. Ernesto has $17.80. If he gets a shirt for $14.90, will he have at least $4.00 left for lunch?

4. Gwen tries to spend less than $10.00 at the mall. If she buys a necklace for $5.75 and a barrette for $2.10, will she keep within her limit?

5. Satoshi paid $5.13 and $4.98 for two pairs of earrings. She had $12.00 when she came to the mall. Does she have $1.00 left for bus fare?

6. Curtis likes two pairs of sneakers. One costs $38.25, and the other, $40.95. Are the prices more than $5.00 different?

7. Miriam has $85.13 in a savings account and wants to keep $50.00 in it. If she buys a jacket for $24.79, will she still have at least $50.00?

8. Samir picks up some items at a drugstore for $3.99, $1.23, and $5.66. About how much did he spend?

Add down. Then check your work by adding up. Use what you know about estimating to decide if your answer is reasonable.

1. $\quad$ 48 352 +216	48 352 +216	2. $\quad$ 5,094 1,731 +2,825	5,094 1,731 +2,825

3. $\quad$ 29,875
4,481
+ 1,793 $\qquad$ 29,875
4,481
+ 1,793

Subtract. Check your answer by adding. Use what you know about estimating to decide if your answer is reasonable.

4. $\quad$ 520
−186
$\overline{\quad 334 \quad}$ $\qquad$ 186
+334

5. $\quad$ 3,601
−2,723 $\qquad$ +

6. $\quad$ 70,245
−49,758 $\qquad$ +

A check **register** shows how much money is in a checking account.

A **payment** is money taken out. It is subtracted from the **balance**.

A **deposit** is money put in. It is added to the balance.

Find the balance by subtracting payments and adding deposits. Circle *add* or *subtract* at each step. Check your work.

No.	Description of Transaction	Payment	Deposit	Balance	
				$ 329 50	Balance
	paycheck	$	$ 215 77	215 77	Add or subtract?
					New balance
421	Old Towne Records	23 56			Add or subtract?
					New balance
422	Chang's Groceries	39 91			Add or subtract?
					New balance
	from Lloyd Arnold		75 90		Add or subtract?
					New balance
423	Bayside Animal Hospital	52 87			Add or subtract?
					New balance

Checking Addition and Subtraction

You can write a number sentence to help you solve a problem.

Renee scored 23,461 points on her favorite video game today. The most points she has ever scored is 26,250. How far was she from her best score today?

Let *n* stand for the number you do not know.

$$26,250 - 23,461 = n$$
$$26,250 - 23,461 = 2,789$$
$$n = 2,789$$

Renee was 2,789 points short of her best score.

Write a number sentence for each problem. Then solve.

1. Cazim spent $21.30 on a computer game last month and $29.66 on another game this month. How much did he spend in two months?

2. Heidi bought a game last week for $32.84. Today it went on sale for $22.95. How much cheaper was it on sale?

3. A puzzle has 5,000 pieces. So far, Alex has put together 3,088 of them. How many pieces are left to put together?

4. A game has 500 question cards. Jeff and Uma used 212 cards playing the game. How many cards did they not use?

5. Zoe scored 14,560 points in the first half of a game and 17,328 points in the second half. How many points did she score in all?

6. A board game costs $29.70, and an extra box of question cards costs $9.95. How much do both cost together?

7. Pedro got $40.00 for his birthday. He spent $19.36 on a game. How much money does he have left?

8. A toy store carries 107 board games, 235 video games, and 163 computer games. How many games does it carry in all?

Multiply to combine groups of the same size.

3 packs × 6 cans = ? cans

$3 \times 6 = 18$ $\begin{array}{r} 6 \\ \times\,3 \\ \hline 18 \end{array}$

Factors   Product

Multiply.

1. $\begin{array}{r} 5 \\ \times\,4 \\ \hline \end{array}$ 2. $\begin{array}{r} 4 \\ \times\,3 \\ \hline \end{array}$ 3. $\begin{array}{r} 6 \\ \times\,5 \\ \hline \end{array}$ 4. $\begin{array}{r} 8 \\ \times\,6 \\ \hline \end{array}$ 5. $\begin{array}{r} 4 \\ \times\,4 \\ \hline \end{array}$ 6. $\begin{array}{r} 7 \\ \times\,2 \\ \hline \end{array}$

7. $\begin{array}{r} 6 \\ \times\,2 \\ \hline \end{array}$ 8. $\begin{array}{r} 9 \\ \times\,4 \\ \hline \end{array}$ 9. $\begin{array}{r} 7 \\ \times\,3 \\ \hline \end{array}$ 10. $\begin{array}{r} 5 \\ \times\,5 \\ \hline \end{array}$ 11. $\begin{array}{r} 9 \\ \times\,7 \\ \hline \end{array}$ 12. $\begin{array}{r} 8 \\ \times\,8 \\ \hline \end{array}$

13. $\begin{array}{r} 8 \\ \times\,5 \\ \hline \end{array}$ 14. $\begin{array}{r} 9 \\ \times\,2 \\ \hline \end{array}$ 15. $\begin{array}{r} 7 \\ \times\,4 \\ \hline \end{array}$ 16. $\begin{array}{r} 8 \\ \times\,3 \\ \hline \end{array}$ 17. $\begin{array}{r} 9 \\ \times\,9 \\ \hline \end{array}$ 18. $\begin{array}{r} 7 \\ \times\,6 \\ \hline \end{array}$

19. $\begin{array}{r} 9 \\ \times\,8 \\ \hline \end{array}$ 20. $\begin{array}{r} 7 \\ \times\,7 \\ \hline \end{array}$ 21. $\begin{array}{r} 6 \\ \times\,6 \\ \hline \end{array}$ 22. $\begin{array}{r} 9 \\ \times\,5 \\ \hline \end{array}$ 23. $\begin{array}{r} 8 \\ \times\,4 \\ \hline \end{array}$ 24. $\begin{array}{r} 9 \\ \times\,3 \\ \hline \end{array}$

Write a multiplication sentence for each group of objects. Then solve.

25.

2 packs of hot dogs
8 hot dogs in a pack
How many hot dogs?

26.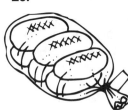

4 bags of rolls
6 rolls in a bag
How many rolls?

27.

8 packs of muffins
3 muffins in a pack
How many muffins?

28.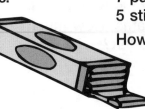

7 packs of gum
5 sticks in a pack
How many sticks of gum?

Multiplication: Basic Facts

Read each property below. Then solve the problems beside it.

COMMUTATIVE PROPERTY

$$\begin{array}{c} 3 \\ \times 4 \\ \hline 12 \end{array}$$ > Factors < $$\begin{array}{c} 4 \\ \times 3 \\ \hline 12 \end{array}$$

← Products →

If the order of the factors changes, the product remains the same.

1. $$\begin{array}{c} 5 \\ \times 4 \end{array} \quad \begin{array}{c} 4 \\ \times 5 \end{array}$$
2. $$\begin{array}{c} 8 \\ \times 2 \end{array} \quad \begin{array}{c} 2 \\ \times 8 \end{array}$$
3. $$\begin{array}{c} 9 \\ \times 6 \end{array} \quad \begin{array}{c} 6 \\ \times 9 \end{array}$$

4. $7 \times 9 = $ _____

5. $3 \times 8 = $ _____

IDENTITY PROPERTY

$$\begin{array}{c} 1 \\ \times 8 \\ \hline 8 \end{array} \quad \begin{array}{c} 7 \\ \times 1 \\ \hline 7 \end{array}$$

If one of two factors is 1, the product is the other factor.

6. $$\begin{array}{c} 1 \\ \times 4 \end{array}$$
7. $$\begin{array}{c} 5 \\ \times 1 \end{array}$$
8. $$\begin{array}{c} 6 \\ \times 1 \end{array}$$
9. $$\begin{array}{c} 1 \\ \times 3 \end{array}$$

10. $9 \times 1 = $ _____

11. $1 \times 2 = $ _____

PROPERTY OF ZERO

$$\begin{array}{c} 0 \\ \times 3 \\ \hline 0 \end{array} \quad \begin{array}{c} 9 \\ \times 0 \\ \hline 0 \end{array}$$

If one of two factors is 0, the product is 0.

12. $$\begin{array}{c} 0 \\ \times 2 \end{array}$$
13. $$\begin{array}{c} 9 \\ \times 0 \end{array}$$
14. $$\begin{array}{c} 4 \\ \times 0 \end{array}$$
15. $$\begin{array}{c} 0 \\ \times 6 \end{array}$$

16. $7 \times 0 = $ _____

17. $0 \times 5 = $ _____

ASSOCIATIVE PROPERTY

$(3 \times 4) \times 2 = 3 \times (4 \times 2)$
$12 \quad \times 2 = 3 \times \quad 8$
$24 = 24$

If the grouping of factors changes, the product remains the same.

18. $(4 \times 2) \times 3 = $ _____ $\times 3 = $ _____

$4 \times (2 \times 3) = 4 \times $ _____ $ = $ _____

19. $5 \times (1 \times 6) = 5 \times $ _____ $ = $ _____

$(5 \times 1) \times 6 = $ _____ $\times 6 = $ _____

Some problems can be solved by making an organized list.

Alaina, Becky, Camille, and Deanna want to go on a roller coaster. Only 2 people can be seated in each car. How many ways can the girls be seated in pairs?

Alaina & Becky
Alaina & Camille
Alaina & Deanna
Becky & Camille
Becky & Deanna
Camille & Deanna

This list shows there are 6 possible pairs of girls.

Make an organized list to solve each problem.

1. Kelvin is interested in 3 equal-priced books, one on animals, one on baseball, and one on caves. He has money for only 2 books. How many combinations of 2 books could he buy?

2. Judges at the fair awarded 1st, 2nd, 3rd, and 4th-place ribbons to 4 different pumpkins. Iris won 2 of these ribbons. How many different combinations of 2 ribbons could she have won?

3. Akio, Brent, Cesar, and Dylan are going canoeing. Only 2 people can fit in a canoe. How many different pairs of boys can there be?

4. Naomi ordered a sugar cone with 2 scoops of ice cream. Each scoop was a different flavor. The available flavors were vanilla, chocolate, strawberry, banana, and cookie dough. How many possible combinations of ice cream could Naomi have had?

Problem Solving: Making an Organized List

Multiply the ones, the tens, and the hundreds. Regroup as often as you need to.

1. (1)
   24
   ×4
   96

2. (4)
   47
   ×6
   282

3. 51
   ×5

4. 15
   ×4

5. 26
   ×9

6. 72
   ×8

7. 75
   ×2

8. 38
   ×9

9. 49
   ×3

10. 86
    ×6

11. 94
    ×8

12. 67
    ×7

13. (2 1)
    176
    ×3
    528

14. (3 2)
    244
    ×7
    1,708

15. 703
    ×4

16. 324
    ×2

17. 243
    ×8

18. 399
    ×5

19. 427
    ×6

20. 296
    ×2

21. 832
    ×7

22. 961
    ×9

23. 407
    ×4

24. 850
    ×9

25. 562
    ×8

26. 973
    ×5

27. 628
    ×3

Multiply to find the total cost of each group of items below.

28. 3 orders of french fries at $0.65 each

29. 9 hot dogs at $1.19 each

30. 4 small lemonades at $0.57 each

31. 8 orders of popcorn at $1.47 each

32. 5 jumbo double burgers at $2.68 each

33. 7 popsicles at $0.92 each

Multiplying Two- and Three-Digit Numbers

23

Multiply. Regroup as often as you need to.

1. $2\ 1$
    $\begin{array}{r} 1,520 \\ \times 5 \\ \hline 7,600 \end{array}$

2. $1\ 1$
    $\begin{array}{r} 9,178 \\ \times 2 \\ \hline 18,356 \end{array}$

3. $\begin{array}{r} 1,096 \\ \times 7 \\ \hline \end{array}$

4. $\begin{array}{r} 3,506 \\ \times 6 \\ \hline \end{array}$

5. $\begin{array}{r} 4,867 \\ \times 4 \\ \hline \end{array}$

6. $\begin{array}{r} 9,315 \\ \times 3 \\ \hline \end{array}$

7. $\begin{array}{r} 5,187 \\ \times 7 \\ \hline \end{array}$

8. $\begin{array}{r} 7,682 \\ \times 5 \\ \hline \end{array}$

9. $\begin{array}{r} 2,593 \\ \times 9 \\ \hline \end{array}$

10. $\begin{array}{r} 8,078 \\ \times 6 \\ \hline \end{array}$

11. $\begin{array}{r} 3,064 \\ \times 8 \\ \hline \end{array}$

12. $\begin{array}{r} 2,320 \\ \times 9 \\ \hline \end{array}$

13. $\begin{array}{r} 8,509 \\ \times 4 \\ \hline \end{array}$

14. $\begin{array}{r} 6,218 \\ \times 3 \\ \hline \end{array}$

15. $\begin{array}{r} 7,419 \\ \times 5 \\ \hline \end{array}$

16. $\begin{array}{r} 10,046 \\ \times 2 \\ \hline \end{array}$

17. $\begin{array}{r} 21,600 \\ \times 6 \\ \hline \end{array}$

18. $\begin{array}{r} 18,418 \\ \times 3 \\ \hline \end{array}$

19. $\begin{array}{r} 97,285 \\ \times 2 \\ \hline \end{array}$

20. $\begin{array}{r} 72,089 \\ \times 5 \\ \hline \end{array}$

21. $\begin{array}{r} 32,624 \\ \times 8 \\ \hline \end{array}$

22. $\begin{array}{r} 28,967 \\ \times 7 \\ \hline \end{array}$

23. $\begin{array}{r} 83,564 \\ \times 9 \\ \hline \end{array}$

Multiply to find the cost of each group of things.

24. 7 shirts at $23.45 each

25. 5 pairs of slacks at $30.73 each

26. 9 jackets at $68.50 each

27. 6 suits at $257.38 each

28. 8 coats at $124.99 each

Sometimes a problem does not contain enough information to solve it.

It costs $4.25 to make a CD of digital pictures. How much will it cost Alfonso to put all the pictures from his vacation on CDs?

You need to know how many CDs
Alfonso needs for his pictures.
Suppose he needs 3 CDs.

$$\begin{array}{r} \$4.25 \\ \times\ 3 \\ \hline \$12.75 \end{array}$$

Read and think about each problem. Write what kind of information is needed to solve it. Then make up a number and solve the problem.

1. Julien shot 4 rolls of film at the national park. How many pictures did he take?

2. A photo album cost $8.95. Mrs. Ramirez bought one album for each of her children. How much did she spend?

3. Only 39 people are in the picture of the Woods family picnic. More than 39 were at the picnic. How many people were not in the picture?

4. Mr. Bentley charges $15.79 to take a child's picture. How much did he charge to take pictures of the Kramer children?

5. In a high-school graduation picture, the students are lined up in rows of 24. How many students are in the picture?

6. A photo enlargement costs either $3.69 or $4.25, depending on the size. How much would 2 enlargements cost?

7. Picture frames were on sale for $2.84 each. Mehri bought one for each of her brothers and sisters. How much did she pay for all of them?

8. Byron bought a photo album and a special pen for photographs. How much did he spend in all?

Divide to break a group into smaller groups of the same size.

Dividend Divisor

$$32 \div 4 = 8 \qquad 4\overline{)32}^{\,8}$$

Quotient

To help you divide or to check your answer, think of multiplication.

$$\begin{array}{r} 4 \\ \times 8 \\ \hline 32 \end{array}$$

Divide. Check by multiplying.

1. $21 \div 3 =$ _____

2. $28 \div 4 =$ _____

3. $18 \div 2 =$ _____

4. $9 \div 9 =$ _____

5. $24 \div 6 =$ _____

6. $64 \div 8 =$ _____

7. $45 \div 5 =$ _____

8. $16 \div 4 =$ _____

9. $49 \div 7 =$ _____

10. $25 \div 5 =$ _____

11. $72 \div 9 =$ _____

12. $24 \div 8 =$ _____

13. $7\overline{)42}$

14. $6\overline{)48}$

15. $9\overline{)36}$

16. $5\overline{)35}$

17. $8\overline{)56}$

18. $8\overline{)40}$

19. $9\overline{)54}$

20. $4\overline{)36}$

21. $6\overline{)30}$

22. $3\overline{)24}$

23. $6\overline{)36}$

24. $8\overline{)16}$

25. $9\overline{)63}$

26. $7\overline{)56}$

27. $5\overline{)10}$

28. $3\overline{)27}$

29. $7\overline{)28}$

30. $5\overline{)40}$

31. $8\overline{)48}$

32. $9\overline{)81}$

33. Bianca has 54 rocks in her collection. If she arranges 9 rocks in a box, how many boxes will she fill?

34. Jake has a collection of 48 fossils. If he stores 6 fossils in each box, how many boxes will he fill?

Division: Basic Facts

Sometimes a number does not divide evenly.

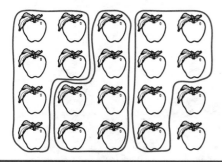

$$6\overline{)20} \quad \begin{array}{r} 3 \text{ R2} \\ \underline{18} \\ 2 \end{array}$$

20 apples

3 groups of 6 apples

2 apples left over

Divide. Write the remainder after the quotient. Check by multiplying, and then adding the remainder to the product.

1. $3\overline{)29}$ $\begin{array}{r}9\text{ R2}\\ \underline{27}\\ 2\end{array}$ $\begin{array}{r}3\\ \times 9\\ \hline 27\\ +\ 2\\ \hline 29\end{array}$

2. $2\overline{)15}$

3. $9\overline{)59}$

4. $7\overline{)30}$

5. $5\overline{)42}$

6. $7\overline{)54}$

7. $4\overline{)37}$

8. $6\overline{)43}$

9. $9\overline{)88}$

10. $4\overline{)22}$

11. $8\overline{)60}$

12. $5\overline{)36}$

13. $6\overline{)27}$

14. $9\overline{)51}$

15. $7\overline{)48}$

16. $4\overline{)19}$

17. $8\overline{)70}$

18. $3\overline{)28}$

19. $8\overline{)31}$

20. $5\overline{)49}$

Sometimes a problem has a remainder.

A bookstore owner wants to talk to 22 publishers at a convention. She can talk to 3 publishers in an hour. How many hours should she allow?

First, divide.

$$3 \overline{)22} \quad \begin{array}{r} 7 \text{ R1} \\ \underline{21} \\ 1 \end{array}$$

Now think.

She can talk to 21 publishers in 7 hours. There is 1 publisher left, so she needs 8 hours.

Solve each problem. Think about the quotient and the remainder. Then answer the question.

1. A group of 44 people went to a book convention. If only 5 people could travel in one car, how many cars were needed?

2. At the convention, 88 publishers set up stands. The stands were in rows of 9. How many rows were there?

3. Pilar signed and sold 21 copies of her book. The copies were packed in boxes of 6. How many boxes did Pilar open? How many copies were left?

4. A publisher sent 41 copies of a book to a store. If 9 books fit in a box, how many boxes were needed?

5. One publisher threw a party for 79 people. They were seated 8 to a table. How many tables were full? How many people sat at the extra table?

6. A publisher set out 50 books in 6 equal piles with the extras in front. How many books were in each pile? How many were in front?

7. Harry had $27. How many $7 books could he buy? How much money would he have left?

8. At one stand, 4 workers shared 18 doughnuts equally. How many did each person get? How many were left?

Problem Solving: Interpreting a Remainder

Divide, multiply, and subtract. Then repeat for the next place value.

1.
$$\begin{array}{r} ^{x24} \\ 4\overline{)96} \\ -8 \\ \hline 16 \\ -16 \\ \hline \end{array}$$
$$\begin{array}{r} 4 \\ x24 \\ \hline 96 \end{array}$$

2. $7\overline{)91}$

3. $5\overline{)505}$

4. $8\overline{)872}$

5. $6\overline{)93}$

6. $4\overline{)764}$

7. $7\overline{)998}$

8. $5\overline{)610}$

Sometimes you must regroup the hundreds as tens before you can divide. Be careful to place the quotient carefully.

$$\begin{array}{r} ^{x82} \\ 6\overline{)492} \\ -48 \\ \hline 12 \\ -12 \\ \hline \end{array}$$

Divide.

9. $5\overline{)225}$

10. $8\overline{)704}$

11. $7\overline{)266}$

12. $9\overline{)846}$

13. $6\overline{)570}$

14. $3\overline{)118}$

15. $5\overline{)369}$

16. $3\overline{)158}$

17. $7\overline{)485}$

18. $9\overline{)653}$

19. Kate has to learn 435 lines for a play in 5 days. How many lines should she learn each day?

20. Ramon folded 868 play programs in 4 hours. He folded the same number each hour. How many did he fold each hour?

Divide. Be careful to place the quotient correctly.

1.
$$
\begin{array}{r}
\$0.87 \\
4\overline{)\$3.48} \\
-3.2 \\
\hline
28 \\
-28 \\
\end{array}
$$

2. $5\overline{)\$4.75}$

3. $7\overline{)\$9.10}$

4. $9\overline{)\$6.66}$

5. $3\overline{)2,508}$

6. $8\overline{)7,228}$

7. $2\overline{)3,410}$

8. $6\overline{)4,524}$

9. $5\overline{)\$23.55}$

10. $7\overline{)\$35.63}$

11. $6\overline{)\$54.90}$

12. $4\overline{)\$83.28}$

13. $2\overline{)12,756}$

14. $8\overline{)24,242}$

15. $4\overline{)37,943}$

16. $9\overline{)63,081}$

17. The scout troop put 3,452 pieces of fudge in bags of 4 pieces. How many bags did they have to sell?

18. Mrs. Oswald paid Isaiah $30.90 for 6 hours work. How much did she pay him per hour?

Dividing Larger Numbers

Sometimes a problem contains more information than you need to solve it.

Mr. Simmons opened an order of 6 magic hats. ~~The hats are in 3 sizes, but~~ they all have the same price. If the order cost $45.00, how much did each hat cost?

You don't need to know the number of sizes. Cross that information out. Then divide to find the price of each hat.

```
       $ 7.50
  6 ) $45.00
       42
        3 0
        3 0
```

Read and think about each problem. Cross out information you do not need. Then solve the problem and check the answer.

1. Ivonna unpacked 56 sets of trick rings. Each set costs $1.56. If 8 sets come in a box, how many boxes did she unpack?

2. Gilbert put 16 magic cups and 12 rope tricks on the shelf. There were 12 magic cups already there. How many magic cups are on the shelf now?

3. The endless scarf trick contains 63 scarves. Each scarf is 15 inches wide. There are 7 scarves of each color in the trick. How many colors are there?

4. A bottle holds 2 ounces of invisible ink. If 42 bottles are arranged in 6 equal rows, how many bottles are in each row?

5. The shop was open a total of 16 days in 4 weeks. It was open the same number of days each week for 6 hours a day. How many days a week was it open?

6. There are 27 Chango-O coins on the shelf. An order for 6 boxes of 8 coins arrived this morning. How many coins were in the order?

7. On Monday, the shop had 64 books about magic. There were 12 books by the same author. That week, 8 books were sold. How many books were left?

8. There are 7 magic wands in the shop. Each one is 36 inches long. Each wand comes apart in 4 equal-sized sections. How long is each section?

1. Before her vacation trip, Mrs. Thornton bought 9 gallons of gas at $2.75 per gallon. How much did she pay in all?

2. Mr. Van Houten paid $3.48 for 6 postcards. How much did each postcard cost?

3. The Shapiros' car used 8 gallons of gas to travel 184 miles. About how many miles did the car travel per gallon?

4. About 2,580 people pass through the gates of Rocky Hill Amusement Park every hour. How many people pass through in 6 hours?

5. The O'Connors paid $63.75 for 5 tickets to the Rodeo Fair. Each ticket was the same price. How much did each one cost?

6. The Luongs budgeted $2,178 for a 9-day vacation trip. How much can they allow themselves to spend per day?

7. Every week, an average of 12,495 people visit the Great Western Caves. About how many people visit them in 4 weeks?

8. Big River State Park has had an average of 250,510 visitors per year for the last 7 years. How many visitors has it had in 7 years?

When 10 is a factor, the product is the other factor with one 0 after it.

When 100 is a factor, the product is the other factor with two 0s after it.

$$\begin{array}{r} 35 \\ \times 10 \\ \hline 350 \end{array} \qquad \begin{array}{r} 100 \\ \times 79 \\ \hline 7{,}900 \end{array}$$

Multiply.

1.
$$\begin{array}{r} 12 \\ \times 10 \\ \hline \end{array}$$

2.
$$\begin{array}{r} 10 \\ \times 43 \\ \hline \end{array}$$

3.
$$\begin{array}{r} 90 \\ \times 10 \\ \hline \end{array}$$

4.
$$\begin{array}{r} 791 \\ \times 10 \\ \hline \end{array}$$

5.
$$\begin{array}{r} 10 \\ \times 107 \\ \hline \end{array}$$

6.
$$\begin{array}{r} 8 \\ \times 100 \\ \hline \end{array}$$

7.
$$\begin{array}{r} 58 \\ \times 100 \\ \hline \end{array}$$

8.
$$\begin{array}{r} 100 \\ \times 82 \\ \hline \end{array}$$

9.
$$\begin{array}{r} 435 \\ \times 100 \\ \hline \end{array}$$

10.
$$\begin{array}{r} 100 \\ \times 510 \\ \hline \end{array}$$

Multiplying by tens or hundreds is like multiplying by ones.

Think of 30 × 24 as 3 × 10 × 24.
Think of 300 × 24 as 3 × 100 × 24.

$$\begin{array}{r} 24 \\ \times 3 \\ \hline 72 \end{array} \qquad \begin{array}{r} 24 \\ \times 30 \\ \hline 720 \end{array} \qquad \begin{array}{r} 24 \\ \times 300 \\ \hline 7{,}200 \end{array}$$

Multiply.

11.
$$\begin{array}{r} 81 \\ \times 30 \\ \hline \end{array}$$

12.
$$\begin{array}{r} 49 \\ \times 60 \\ \hline \end{array}$$

13.
$$\begin{array}{r} 68 \\ \times 50 \\ \hline \end{array}$$

14.
$$\begin{array}{r} 76 \\ \times 80 \\ \hline \end{array}$$

15.
$$\begin{array}{r} 92 \\ \times 70 \\ \hline \end{array}$$

16.
$$\begin{array}{r} 28 \\ \times 600 \\ \hline \end{array}$$

17.
$$\begin{array}{r} 163 \\ \times 90 \\ \hline \end{array}$$

18.
$$\begin{array}{r} 32 \\ \times 400 \\ \hline \end{array}$$

19.
$$\begin{array}{r} 839 \\ \times 20 \\ \hline \end{array}$$

20.
$$\begin{array}{r} 41 \\ \times 900 \\ \hline \end{array}$$

21.
$$\begin{array}{r} 926 \\ \times 200 \\ \hline \end{array}$$

22.
$$\begin{array}{r} 508 \\ \times 800 \\ \hline \end{array}$$

23.
$$\begin{array}{r} 809 \\ \times 300 \\ \hline \end{array}$$

24.
$$\begin{array}{r} 745 \\ \times 500 \\ \hline \end{array}$$

25.
$$\begin{array}{r} 612 \\ \times 700 \\ \hline \end{array}$$

---

26. About 50 planes take off from the airport every hour. About how many planes take off in 24 hours?

27. Air Food Service supplies meals to 600 planes a day. Each plane gets an average of 256 meals. How many meals is that in all?

Think of 26 as 20 + 6.
Multiply by the ones: 6 × 74 = 444
Multiply by the tens: 20 × 74 = 1,480
Add the products: 444 + 1,480 = 1,924

```
    74
  × 26
   444
  1480
 1,924
```

Multiply.

1. $\begin{array}{r} 67 \\ \times 32 \end{array}$ (30 + 2)

2. $\begin{array}{r} 83 \\ \times 15 \end{array}$

3. $\begin{array}{r} 45 \\ \times 64 \end{array}$

4. $\begin{array}{r} 21 \\ \times 48 \end{array}$

5. $\begin{array}{r} 91 \\ \times 76 \end{array}$

6. $\begin{array}{r} 72 \\ \times 29 \end{array}$

7. $\begin{array}{r} 27 \\ \times 87 \end{array}$

8. $\begin{array}{r} 56 \\ \times 71 \end{array}$

9. $\begin{array}{r} 19 \\ \times 95 \end{array}$

10. $\begin{array}{r} 85 \\ \times 34 \end{array}$

11. $\begin{array}{r} 183 \\ \times 53 \end{array}$

12. $\begin{array}{r} 452 \\ \times 18 \end{array}$

13. $\begin{array}{r} 605 \\ \times 84 \end{array}$

14. $\begin{array}{r} 271 \\ \times 42 \end{array}$

15. $\begin{array}{r} 917 \\ \times 67 \end{array}$

16. $\begin{array}{r} 1,746 \\ \times 76 \end{array}$

17. $\begin{array}{r} 2,368 \\ \times 95 \end{array}$

18. $\begin{array}{r} 4,494 \\ \times 39 \end{array}$

19. $\begin{array}{r} 6,530 \\ \times 83 \end{array}$

20. $\begin{array}{r} 3,809 \\ \times 48 \end{array}$

21. Ms. Jankowitz earns $18.72 an hour as a welder. She works 36 hours a week. How much does she earn in a week?

22. Mr. Diaz works 28 hours a week in a metal shop. He earns $19.08 an hour. How much does he earn at the metal shop in a week?

Multiplying by Two-Digit Numbers

```
  276
×239
 2484
 8280
55200
65,964
```

Think of 239 as 200 + 30 + 9.
Multiply by the ones: 9 × 276 = 2,484
Multiply by the tens: 30 × 276 = 8,280
Multiply by the hundreds: 200 × 276 = 55,200
Then add the products.

Multiply.

1. 826
   ×174

2. 742
   ×209

3. 480
   ×683

4. 365
   ×715

5. 914
   ×521

6. 310
   ×936

7. 650
   ×705

8. 879
   ×243

9. 422
   ×198

10. 582
   ×847

11. It cost $7.50 to enter a cat in the cat show. If 213 cats were entered, how much money was collected on entry fees?

12. A ticket to the cat show cost $8.75. On the first day, 890 tickets were sold. How much money was collected on the tickets?

13. Valerie makes cat name tags. She sold 648 tags for $4.95 each. How much money did she take in?

14. Neal sold T-shirts at the cat show for $9.32 each. He sold 967 T-shirts in one day. How much money did Neal collect?

Sometimes the solution to a problem takes two or more steps.

Rocco's band rehearsed 7 hours last week. This week, the band rehearsed 3 hours on Monday, 2 hours on Tuesday, 4 hours on Wednesday, and 4 hours on Thursday. How many more hours did the band rehearse this week than last?

First, add.   Then subtract.

3 + 2 + 4 + 4 = 13 hours   13 − 7 = 6 hours

Read each problem. Think about the two steps needed to solve it. Then solve the problem and check the answer.

1. The lead guitarist made a $100 down payment on a new guitar. He will pay the rest in 8 equal installments of $60. How much will the guitar cost in all?

2. The band was paid $300 for playing a job. Of that amount, $30 went to the agent who got the job for the band. The rest was split evenly among the 5 band members. How much did each band member get?

3. The band knows 45 songs. It played 12 songs in the first set, 15 songs in the second set, and 11 songs in the last set. If no songs were repeated, how many songs does the band know that it didn't play?

4. The drummer drove 18 miles to pick up the singer and then another 28 miles to the job. The rest of the band drove 52 miles to the job. Who drove farther and by how much?

5. The singer made $54 for a 3-hour job on Friday night and $60 for a 4-hour job on Saturday. Which job paid better per hour? How much better?

Problem Solving: Planning Two-Step Solutions

Dividing by tens is like dividing by ones. Study each example below, and then solve the problems to the right of it. Be careful to place the quotient correctly.

```
      4 R5
20 ) 85      Think:       1.  30 ) 96      2.  20 ) 68      3.  40 ) 87
     80      85 ÷ 20
      5
```

```
      5 R39
70 ) 389     Think:       4.  50 ) 206     5.  60 ) 400     6.  80 ) 720
    350      389 ÷ 70
     39
```

```
     32
30 ) 960     Think:       7.  20 ) 660     8.  30 ) 753     9.  70 ) 910
     90      96 ÷ 30
     60
     60
```

```
      41
80 ) 3,280   Think:      10.  90 ) 6,571  11.  50 ) 3,149  12.  80 ) 4,640
    3 20     328 ÷ 80
      80
      80
```

```
     434 R4
20 ) 8,684   Think:      13.  40 ) 8,369  14.  60 ) 9,902  15.  30 ) 6,420
     8 0      86 ÷ 20
      68
      60
      84
      80
       4
```

To divide by tens and ones, round the divisor to the nearest ten and estimate.

61 is about 60
429 ÷ 60 is like **42 ÷ 6,** or about 7
Now multiply: 7 × 61 = 427
Subtract: 429 − 427 = 2

$$61\overline{)429} \quad \begin{array}{r} 7\ R2 \\ \end{array}$$

```
     7 R2
61 ) 429
     427
       2
```

```
   61
  × 7
  427
 +  2
  429
```

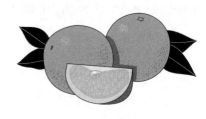

Divide. Check by multiplying. Remember to add any remainder.

1. $38\overline{)245}$ Think: **245 ÷ 40**

2. $73\overline{)300}$ Think: **300 ÷ 70**

3. $82\overline{)436}$ Think: **436 ÷ 80**

4. $63\overline{)567}$

5. $47\overline{)405}$

6. $19\overline{)151}$

7. $42\overline{)252}$

8. $94\overline{)290}$

9. $56\overline{)542}$

10. $28\overline{)240}$

11. $71\overline{)355}$

12. $59\overline{)500}$

13. $67\overline{)288}$

14. $92\overline{)621}$

15. $84\overline{)756}$

16. Today, 168 kilograms of oranges were delivered to the fruit market. How many 21-kilogram cases were delivered?

17. Fernando unpacked 216 heads of lettuce. If 36 heads are in a case, how many cases did he unpack?

Dividing by Two-Digit Numbers: One-Digit Quotients

The quotient has **two** digits because 10 × 78 = 780 and 100 × 78 = 7,800.

```
        42 R10
78 ) 3,286
     3 1 2
       166
       156
        10
```

First, find the tens. There are 328 tens in 3,286, and 78 is about 80.

　　328 ÷ 80 is like **32 ÷ 8**, or about **4**
Write 4 in the **tens** place. Multiply and subtract. Bring down the ones.

Now find the ones. There are 166 ones.
　　166 ÷ 80 is like **16 ÷ 8**, or about **2**
Write 2 in the **ones** place. Multiply and subtract.

Divide. Check by multiplying. Remember to add any remainder.

1. 42) 950

2. 18) 414

3. 29) 900

4. 57) 741

5. 63) 2,840

6. 84) 2,352

7. 92) 6,495

8. 27) 1,809

9. 52) 3,908

10. 65) 2,549

11. 39) 3,471

12. 91) 1,638

13. Uptown Bakery made 5,976 cookies today. If 72 cookies were put in a bag, how many bags were filled?

14. Lynette can make 1,128 doughnuts from a batch of dough. She can pack 12 doughnuts in a box. How many boxes can Lynette fill with a batch of dough?

The quotient has **three** digits because 100 × 54 = 5,400 and 1,000 × 54 = 54,000.

```
        218
54 ) 11,772
    10 8
       97
       54
      432
      432
```

First, find the hundreds. There are 117 hundreds in 11,772, and 54 is about 50.

     117 ÷ 50 is like **11 ÷ 5,** or about 2

Write 2 in the **hundreds** place. Multiply and subtract. Bring down the tens.

Repeat the steps to find the tens and ones.

Divide. Check by multiplying. Remember to add any remainder.

1. 32) 4,504

2. 41) 9,677

3. 53) 5,671

4. 69) 10,490

5. 28) 18,063

6. 75) 72,225

7. 17) $154.36

8. 92) $227.24

9. 58) $330.60

Dividing by Two-Digit Numbers: Larger Quotients

Estimate products and quotients by rounding
the numbers before multiplying or dividing.

$\begin{array}{r} 471 \\ \times 743 \\ \hline \end{array}$ 700 times 500
is 350,000.
So the answer
is about 350,000.

$29\overline{\smash{)}1{,}189}$ 1,200 divided by
30 is 40. So
the answer is
about 40.

Estimate each answer. Then solve the problem and compare answers.

1. $\begin{array}{r} 37 \\ \times 64 \\ \hline \end{array}$ about

2. $68\overline{\smash{)}6{,}324}$ about

3. $\begin{array}{r} 923 \\ \times 887 \\ \hline \end{array}$ about

4. $\begin{array}{r} 620 \\ \times 29 \\ \hline \end{array}$ about

5. $42\overline{\smash{)}2{,}436}$ about

6. $89\overline{\smash{)}5{,}518}$ about

7. $\begin{array}{r} 397 \\ \times 81 \\ \hline \end{array}$ about

8. $57\overline{\smash{)}6{,}384}$ about

9. $38\overline{\smash{)}20{,}102}$ about

10. This evening, 73 people
ordered egg foo young at
the Golden Dragon. One
order cost $4.89. How
much did the restaurant take
in on this dish?

11. A banquet for 32 people
cost $825.60. Each
person paid the same
amount. How much was
each person's share?

1. There are 672 campers and 42 counselors at Camp Walkamuck. How many campers and counselors are there in all?

2. Horseback-riding lessons cost $28.95 each. How much did Raul pay for 25 lessons?

3. A large can contains 58 servings of beans. Last week, campers ate 1,972 servings of beans. How many cans were used?

4. A total of 296 people signed up to go on the mountain hike. Each leader can take only 37 people. How many leaders are needed?

5. Lake Chilblain is 78 meters wide at one place. Leila swam across the lake there 42 times. How many meters did she swim in all?

6. The sailing classes took 132 people. If 186 people wanted to take the class, how many people were disappointed?

7. A 21-day meal ticket at the camp costs $204.75. How much do meals cost per day?

8. The campers ate 114 cases of hot dogs this summer. If a case contains 576 hot dogs, how many hot dogs did they eat in all?

Problem Solving: Using the Four Operations

When a number sentence has more than one operation, do them in the following order.

1. First, do the work inside parentheses.
2. Next, multiply and divide from left to right.
3. Finally, add and subtract from left to right.

Follow the order of operations to find out which frog won the Frivolous Frog Race. Circle the frog with the highest number of points.

1. Ribert Redford

$7 \times 7 + 81 \div (12 - 3) =$

2. Lillian Pad

$(36 \div 4) + (9 \times 8) - 1 =$

3. Hopalong Cathy

$56 \div (8 - 1) + 8 \times 3 =$

4. Davey Croaket

$(4 + 50) \div (21 - 18) \times 2 =$

5. Tad Paul

$(33 + 12) \div (3 \times 3) - 2 =$

6. Leapin' Lois

$30 - (35 \div 5) \times (2 + 2) =$

7. Sigmund Frog

$(9 - 3) \times (64 \div 8) + 12 =$

8. Jumping Judy

$(72 \div 9) + 5 \times (20 - 15) =$

A **multiple** of a number is the product of that number and any whole number.

Multiples of 6: 6, 12, 18, 24, 30, 36, ...
Multiples of 9: 9, 18, 27, 36, 45, ...

The **common multiples** of 6 and 9 are 18 and 36.

Their **least common multiple** is 18.

List the first ten multiples of each number.

1. 2 _____

2. 3 _____

3. 4 _____

4. 5 _____

5. 6 _____

6. 7 _____

7. 8 _____

8. 9 _____

9. 10 _____

Use your work above to find the common multiples of each group of numbers. Circle the least common multiple of each group.

10. 2, 3 _____

11. 3, 4 _____

12. 4, 5 _____

13. 4, 6 _____

14. 3, 9 _____

15. 6, 8 _____

16. 6, 10 _____

17. 2, 3, 4 _____

18. 3, 4, 8 _____

Finding Multiples

The **factors** of a number are the numbers by which it can be divided evenly.

Factors of 8: 1, 2, 4, and 8
Factors of 12: 1, 2, 3, 4, 6, and 12

The **common factors** of 8 and 12 are 1, 2, and 4.
Their **greatest common factor** is 4.

List the factors of each number.

1. 6 _____
2. 9 _____
3. 10 _____
4. 15 _____
5. 16 _____
6. 18 _____
7. 20 _____
8. 24 _____
9. 30 _____

10. 35 _____
11. 36 _____
12. 40 _____
13. 42 _____
14. 45 _____
15. 48 _____
16. 50 _____
17. 54 _____
18. 64 _____

Use your work above to find the common factors of each set of numbers. Circle the greatest common factor.

19. 6, 8 _____
20. 8, 24 _____
21. 9, 12 _____
22. 12, 16 _____
23. 15, 18 _____
24. 18, 24 _____
25. 18, 48 _____
26. 20, 36 _____
27. 36, 45 _____

A prime number has exactly two factors, 1 and itself. For example, 7 is a prime number. Its only factors are 1 and 7.

$$7 = 1 \times 7$$

A composite number has more than two factors. For example, 12 is a composite number. Its factors are 1, 2, 3, 4, 6, and 12.

$$12 = 1 \times 12$$
$$12 = 2 \times 6$$
$$12 = 3 \times 4$$

Find all the factors of each number below. Then write *prime* or *composite* to describe it.

1. **4:** 1, 2, 4 _____composite_____

2. **5:** _____

3. **6:** _____

4. **8:** _____

5. **10:** _____

6. **11:** _____

7. **13:** _____

8. **15:** _____

A composite number can be shown as the product of prime numbers using a **factor tree**. These factor trees show the **prime factorization** of 12. Notice that the bottom lines are the same.

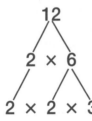 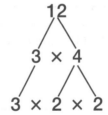

12
2 × 6
2 × 2 × 3

12
3 × 4
3 × 2 × 2

Complete each factor tree.

9.
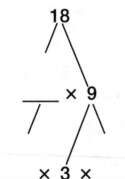
18
____ × 9
____ × 3 × ____

10.
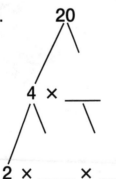
20
4 × ____
2 × ____ × ____

11.
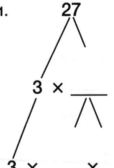
27
3 × ____
3 × ____ × ____

12.
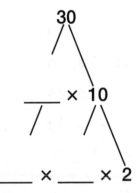
30
____ × 10
____ × ____ × 2

Prime and Composite Numbers

Some problems can be solved by guessing the answer and checking the guess against the clues in the problem.

A scientist found a dinosaur egg. Its length in inches is a one-digit number. The number is composite. It is divisible by both 2 and 3. What is the length?

Guess 8 and check. Is 8 composite? Yes. Is it divisible by 2? Yes. By 3? No. Guess another number. Is 6 composite? Yes. Is it divisible by 2 and by 3? Yes. So the length is 6 inches.

Make a guess and check it to solve each problem.

1. Deinonychus was a type of small dinosaur. Its length in feet is a one-digit number. This number is divisible by 3. It is not a prime and it is not divisible by 2. What is the length?

2. Some scientists think Deinonychus could run as fast as an ostrich. This speed in miles per hour is a two-digit number less than 50. The sum of the digits is 11. The difference between the digits is 5. What is the speed?

3. Tyrannosaurus Rex was a huge dinosaur. The height in feet of one skeleton is a two-digit number that is divisible by 2. The sum of the digits is 6. The digit in the tens place is twice as large as the digit in the ones place. What is the height?

4. The Apatosaurus and the Stegosaurus lived about the same time. The length in feet of the Apatosaurus is 4 times the length of the Stegosaurus. The sum of the lengths is 100. What are the lengths?

Cole ate 3 apples.
There were 8 apples.

$\frac{3}{8}$

The **numerator** tells how many parts are being talked about.

The **denominator** tells how many equal parts there are.

Write the fraction that tells what part is shaded.

1.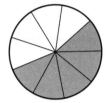

_____

2.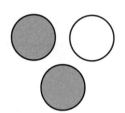

_____

3.

_____

4.

_____

5.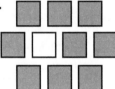

_____

6.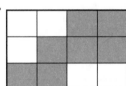

_____

7.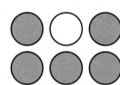

_____

8.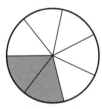

_____

Solve.

9. Piao ate 5 of 12 doughnuts. What fraction of them did he eat?

10. Phoebe walked 8 miles of a 15-mile walkathon. What fraction of the distance did she walk?

11. Raj read 7 of 11 books he took home from the library. What fraction did he read?

12. Elsa has 4 of the New Earth Rock Band's 9 CDs. What part does she have?

13. Will got 81 of 100 answers correct on the test. What fraction did he get correct?

14. Josefa made 13 phone calls this week. There were 4 long-distance calls. What part were long-distance?

Fractions

Equivalent fractions name the same part of a whole or set in different terms.

$$\frac{2}{3} = \frac{2 \times 2}{3 \times 2} = \frac{4}{6}$$

To find an equivalent fraction, multiply the numerator and the denominator by the same number.

Write equivalent fractions.

1.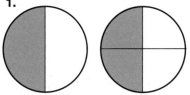

$$\frac{1}{2} = \frac{1 \times 2}{2 \times 2} = \frac{2}{4}$$

2.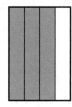

$$\frac{3}{4} = \frac{3 \times}{4 \times} = \frac{}{8}$$

3.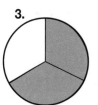

$$\frac{2}{3} = \frac{2 \times}{3 \times} = \frac{}{9}$$

4. $\frac{1}{2} = \frac{1 \times 4}{2 \times 4} = \frac{}{8}$

5. $\frac{2}{5} = \frac{2 \times}{5 \times 2} = \frac{}{10}$

6. $\frac{5}{7} = \frac{5 \times}{7 \times} = \frac{}{21}$

7. $\frac{3}{4} = \frac{}{12}$

8. $\frac{2}{9} = \frac{}{18}$

9. $\frac{4}{5} = \frac{}{15}$

10. $\frac{1}{2} = \frac{}{14}$

11. $\frac{5}{6} = \frac{}{24}$

12. $\frac{2}{3} = \frac{}{12}$

13. $\frac{3}{4} = \frac{}{16}$

14. $\frac{1}{2} = \frac{}{10}$

15. $\frac{3}{8} = \frac{}{24}$

16. $\frac{4}{5} = \frac{}{20}$

Write equivalent fractions with the same denominators for each pair of fractions below.

17. $\frac{1}{2} = \frac{}{6}$ $\frac{1}{3} = \frac{}{6}$

18. $\frac{3}{5} = \frac{}{10}$ $\frac{1}{2} = \frac{}{}$

19. $\frac{2}{3} = \frac{}{12}$ $\frac{3}{4} = \frac{}{}$

20. $\frac{3}{5} = \frac{}{15}$ $\frac{1}{3} = \frac{}{}$

21. $\frac{5}{6} = \frac{}{18}$ $\frac{7}{9} = \frac{}{}$

Complete each problem with an equivalent fraction.

22. Stella watered $\frac{1}{3}$ of the plants. She watered $\frac{}{36}$ of them.

23. Hitoshi sold $\frac{5}{8}$ of the trees on sale at the nursery. He sold $\frac{}{24}$ of the trees.

$$\frac{12}{36} = \frac{12 \div 2}{36 \div 2} = \frac{6}{18}$$

To find an equivalent fraction in **lower terms,** divide the numerator and denominator by the same number.

$$\frac{12}{36} = \frac{12 \div 12}{36 \div 12} = \frac{1}{3}$$

Divide by the largest possible number to find a fraction in **lowest terms.**

Write an equivalent fraction in lower terms.

1. $\frac{16}{28} = \frac{16 \div 2}{28 \div 2} = \frac{8}{14}$

2. $\frac{8}{12} = \frac{8 \div}{12 \div} = \frac{}{6}$

3. $\frac{6}{18} = \frac{6 \div}{18 \div} = \frac{}{6}$

4. $\frac{18}{24} = \frac{}{8}$

5. $\frac{16}{20} = \frac{}{10}$

6. $\frac{24}{36} = \frac{}{9}$

7. $\frac{32}{48} = \frac{}{12}$

8. $\frac{42}{56} = \frac{}{8}$

Write an equivalent fraction in lowest terms.

9. $\frac{8}{12} = \frac{8 \div}{12 \div} = \frac{}{3}$

10. $\frac{6}{24} = \frac{6 \div}{24 \div} = \frac{}{4}$

11. $\frac{12}{20} = \frac{12 \div}{20 \div} = \frac{}{5}$

12. $\frac{6}{12} = \frac{}{2}$

13. $\frac{3}{24} = \frac{}{8}$

14. $\frac{12}{15} = \frac{}{5}$

15. $\frac{9}{12} = \frac{}{4}$

16. $\frac{6}{36} = \frac{}{6}$

17. $\frac{12}{16} = \text{---}$

18. $\frac{5}{10} = \text{---}$

19. $\frac{20}{30} = \text{---}$

20. $\frac{10}{25} = \text{---}$

21. $\frac{16}{48} = \text{---}$

22. $\frac{16}{24} = \text{---}$

23. $\frac{21}{28} = \text{---}$

24. $\frac{24}{40} = \text{---}$

25. $\frac{20}{32} = \text{---}$

26. $\frac{36}{42} = \text{---}$

Complete each problem with an equivalent fraction in lowest terms.

27. On Karina's map, $\frac{10}{16}$ inch represents one mile. In other words, —— inch equals one mile.

28. Andre lives $\frac{8}{10}$ mile from his best friend, Elijah. Elijah lives —— mile away.

Simplifying Fractions

$$\frac{3}{9} + \frac{4}{9} = \frac{3+4}{9} = \frac{7}{9}$$

To add or subtract fractions with like denominators, add or subtract the **numerators**. The denominator stays the same.

Add or subtract. Write each answer in lowest terms.

1. $\frac{3}{7} + \frac{2}{7} = \frac{3+2}{7} = \frac{}{7}$

2. $\frac{7}{9} - \frac{2}{9} = \frac{7-2}{9} = \frac{}{9}$

3. $\frac{1}{10} + \frac{3}{10} + \frac{2}{10} =$

4. $\frac{8}{12} - \frac{5}{12} =$

5. $\frac{4}{6} + \frac{1}{6} =$

6. $\frac{6}{8} - \frac{1}{8} =$

7. $\frac{7}{12} + \frac{1}{12} =$

8. $\frac{19}{20} - \frac{3}{20} =$

9. $\begin{array}{r} \frac{3}{8} \\ + \frac{3}{8} \\ \hline \end{array}$

10. $\begin{array}{r} \frac{7}{21} \\ \frac{5}{21} \\ + \frac{2}{21} \\ \hline \end{array}$

11. $\begin{array}{r} \frac{3}{4} \\ - \frac{1}{4} \\ \hline \end{array}$

12. $\begin{array}{r} \frac{15}{24} \\ - \frac{5}{24} \\ \hline \end{array}$

13. $\begin{array}{r} \frac{7}{30} \\ \frac{1}{30} \\ + \frac{2}{30} \\ \hline \end{array}$

14. $\begin{array}{r} \frac{1}{10} \\ + \frac{7}{10} \\ \hline \end{array}$

15. $\begin{array}{r} \frac{5}{12} \\ - \frac{1}{12} \\ \hline \end{array}$

16. $\begin{array}{r} \frac{13}{15} \\ - \frac{8}{15} \\ \hline \end{array}$

17. $\begin{array}{r} \frac{4}{18} \\ + \frac{5}{18} \\ \hline \end{array}$

18. $\begin{array}{r} \frac{16}{35} \\ - \frac{9}{35} \\ \hline \end{array}$

19. Terrence washed $\frac{2}{9}$ of the windows. Lawrence did $\frac{3}{9}$ of them. What part of the windows have the brothers washed?

20. Erica has $\frac{7}{12}$ of the fence left to paint. If she paints $\frac{3}{12}$ of it this morning, how much will she have left to paint?

To add fractions with unlike denominators, first change the fractions to equivalent fractions with **like** denominators. Then add.

$$\frac{1}{6} = \frac{2}{12}$$
$$+ \frac{3}{4} = \frac{9}{12}$$
$$\frac{11}{12}$$

Find equivalent fractions. Then add. Write each sum in lowest terms.

1. $\frac{1}{2} =$
   $+ \frac{1}{4} =$ ___

2. $\frac{2}{3}$
   $+ \frac{1}{6}$

3. $\frac{4}{9}$
   $+ \frac{1}{3}$

4. $\frac{1}{2}$
   $+ \frac{1}{8}$

5. $\frac{5}{14}$
   $+ \frac{1}{2}$

6. $\frac{9}{16}$
   $+ \frac{1}{4}$

7. $\frac{3}{5}$
   $+ \frac{4}{15}$

8. $\frac{1}{12}$
   $+ \frac{3}{4}$

9. $\frac{3}{7}$
   $+ \frac{1}{3}$

10. $\frac{2}{5}$
    $+ \frac{2}{4}$

11. $\frac{1}{4}$
    $+ \frac{1}{3}$

12. $\frac{4}{5}$
    $+ \frac{1}{6}$

13. $\frac{1}{9}$
    $+ \frac{5}{6}$

14. $\frac{1}{6}$
    $+ \frac{3}{4}$

15. $\frac{3}{8}$
    $+ \frac{4}{7}$

16. $\frac{1}{4}$
    $+ \frac{7}{10}$

17. Nicole used $\frac{1}{4}$ of a bag of charcoal today and $\frac{3}{8}$ of a bag yesterday. How much has she used in all?

18. Chicken cooked in $\frac{7}{10}$ hour. Hot dogs took $\frac{1}{6}$ hour. How long did it take to cook both batches of food?

Adding Fractions with Unlike Denominators

To subtract fractions with unlike denominators, first change the fractions to equivalent fractions with **like** denominators. Then subtract.

$$\begin{array}{r} \frac{5}{9} = \frac{10}{18} \\ -\ \frac{1}{6} = \frac{3}{18} \\ \hline \frac{7}{18} \end{array}$$

Find equivalent fractions. Then subtract. Write each difference in lowest terms.

1. $\frac{2}{3} =$
   $-\ \frac{1}{6} =$ _____

2. $\frac{3}{5}$
   $-\ \frac{3}{10}$

3. $\frac{7}{8}$
   $-\ \frac{1}{4}$

4. $\frac{1}{3}$
   $-\ \frac{2}{9}$

5. $\frac{11}{12}$
   $-\ \frac{2}{3}$

6. $\frac{4}{5}$
   $-\ \frac{7}{15}$

7. $\frac{3}{4}$
   $-\ \frac{11}{20}$

8. $\frac{9}{16}$
   $-\ \frac{3}{8}$

9. $\frac{1}{2}$
   $-\ \frac{2}{7}$

10. $\frac{2}{3}$
    $-\ \frac{1}{4}$

11. $\frac{9}{10}$
    $-\ \frac{9}{15}$

12. $\frac{5}{6}$
    $-\ \frac{4}{9}$

13. $\frac{1}{4}$
    $-\ \frac{1}{6}$

14. $\frac{5}{7}$
    $-\ \frac{1}{3}$

15. $\frac{3}{4}$
    $-\ \frac{1}{10}$

16. $\frac{7}{8}$
    $-\ \frac{5}{6}$

17. Stefan usually practices piano $\frac{9}{10}$ hour each day. Today, he practiced $\frac{1}{2}$ hour. How much more does he have to practice?

18. Sari practiced a new song for $\frac{8}{9}$ hour and an old song $\frac{1}{6}$ hour. How much longer did she practice the new song?

Subtracting Fractions with Unlike Denominators

Read and solve each problem. Write each answer in lowest terms.

1. For the gorilla, $\frac{3}{12}$ of its meal is oranges and $\frac{1}{12}$ is bananas. What part of the meal is fruit?

2. This year, $\frac{4}{9}$ of the zebras had babies and $\frac{1}{9}$ had twins. The rest had one baby. What part had only one baby?

3. The zoo vet checked $\frac{1}{3}$ of the monkeys in the morning and $\frac{3}{5}$ of them in the afternoon. What part did she check?

4. The male lion ate $\frac{7}{10}$ of his food right away. The female lion ate $\frac{7}{8}$ of hers. How much more did the female lion eat?

5. Parrots make up $\frac{11}{24}$ of all the zoo's birds. Of the birds, $\frac{5}{24}$ are Amazon parrots. What part of the birds are other parrots?

6. There was $\frac{2}{3}$ ton of grain this morning. After the feeding, $\frac{1}{7}$ ton remained. How much did the animals eat?

7. Of the bears, $\frac{4}{7}$ are brown bears and $\frac{2}{5}$ are polar bears. What part of the bears are brown or polar bears?

8. At the zoo, $\frac{5}{16}$ of the animals are from Africa and $\frac{1}{4}$ are from Asia. What part of the animals are from these two continents?

Problem Solving: Using Fractions

A fraction can name a number equal to a whole number or a mixed number.

To change a fraction to a mixed number, divide the numerator by the denominator.

$$\frac{7}{3} = 3\overline{)7}\ \ 2\frac{1}{3}$$
$$\frac{6}{1}$$

Change each fraction to a whole number or a mixed number in lowest terms.

1. $\frac{5}{2}$ =

2. $\frac{13}{5}$ =

3. $\frac{8}{4}$ =

4. $\frac{9}{6}$ =

5. $\frac{11}{4}$ =

6. $\frac{12}{3}$ =

7. $\frac{8}{5}$ =

8. $\frac{9}{2}$ =

9. $\frac{7}{6}$ =

10. $\frac{15}{7}$ =

11. $\frac{8}{3}$ =

12. $\frac{10}{2}$ =

13. $\frac{18}{6}$ =

14. $\frac{21}{9}$ =

15. $\frac{19}{4}$ =

16. $\frac{20}{3}$ =

17. $\frac{35}{7}$ =

18. $\frac{15}{6}$ =

19. Claudia practiced her flute $\frac{7}{4}$ hours today. She practiced

_____ hours.

20. Greg's band rehearsed $\frac{9}{3}$ hours this evening. It

rehearsed _____ hours.

21. Jesse spent $\frac{40}{6}$ hours writing a new song this week.

He spent _____ hours writing it.

Mixed Numbers

55

To change a mixed number to a fraction, first multiply the whole number by the denominator.

Add the product and the numerator.

Write the sum over the denominator.

$5\frac{3}{4} \rightarrow 4 \times 5 = 20$

$20 + 3 = 23$

$\frac{23}{4}$

Rename each mixed number as a fraction.

1. $4\frac{+1}{\times 3} =$

2. $1\frac{7}{12} =$

3. $5\frac{1}{6} =$

4. $8\frac{2}{5} =$

5. $6\frac{2}{3} =$

6. $9\frac{1}{4} =$

7. $2\frac{9}{10} =$

8. $3\frac{7}{15} =$

9. $4\frac{4}{7} =$

10. $8\frac{5}{8} =$

11. $5\frac{5}{12} =$

12. $3\frac{13}{24} =$

13. $4\frac{5}{6} =$

14. $3\frac{1}{2} =$

15. $1\frac{3}{8} =$

16. $2\frac{4}{5} =$

17. $1\frac{7}{9} =$

18. $7\frac{3}{4} =$

19. Myra has $6\frac{1}{4}$ bags of candy corn.

She has $\frac{}{4}$ bags.

20. Rishad used $2\frac{1}{3}$ cups of frosting to decorate cupcakes. He used $\frac{}{3}$ cups.

Changing Mixed Numbers to Fractions

To compare fractions with like denominators, look at the numerators.

$$\frac{4}{5} > \frac{3}{5}$$

If the fractions have unlike denominators, change them to equivalent fractions first.

$$\frac{2}{3} < \frac{5}{6} \text{ because } \frac{4}{6} < \frac{5}{6}$$

Compare. Write >, <, or =.

1. $\frac{1}{4}$ ◯ $\frac{2}{8}$

2. $\frac{2}{6}$ ◯ $\frac{1}{2}$

3. $1\frac{4}{5}$ ◯ $2\frac{1}{5}$

4. $\frac{5}{9}$ ◯ $\frac{4}{9}$

5. $\frac{3}{4}$ ◯ $\frac{2}{3}$

6. $3\frac{2}{3}$ ◯ $3\frac{1}{3}$

7. $\frac{5}{6}$ ◯ $\frac{7}{8}$

8. $\frac{11}{12}$ ◯ $\frac{7}{12}$

9. $4\frac{5}{8}$ ◯ $3\frac{7}{8}$

10. $\frac{9}{12}$ ◯ $\frac{3}{4}$

11. $\frac{7}{10}$ ◯ $\frac{3}{5}$

12. $2\frac{1}{3}$ ◯ $1\frac{7}{9}$

13. $\frac{5}{10}$ ◯ $\frac{6}{10}$

14. $\frac{1}{2}$ ◯ $\frac{7}{14}$

15. $5\frac{2}{7}$ ◯ $5\frac{1}{3}$

16. $\frac{3}{8}$ ◯ $\frac{1}{6}$

17. $\frac{7}{9}$ ◯ $\frac{5}{6}$

18. $2\frac{1}{2}$ ◯ $2\frac{5}{10}$

19. For breakfast, the Phelps family ate $\frac{1}{2}$ dozen eggs and $\frac{6}{12}$ dozen muffins. Which did they eat more of?

_____

20. A pancake recipe calls for $1\frac{1}{4}$ cups of sugar. A coffeecake recipe calls for $1\frac{1}{3}$ cups of sugar. Which calls for less sugar?

Add or subtract. Write each answer as a whole number or a mixed number in lowest terms.

1. $\dfrac{5}{8}$
$+ \dfrac{5}{8}$

$\dfrac{10}{8} = 1\dfrac{1}{4}$

2. $\dfrac{11}{6}$
$- \dfrac{5}{6}$

3. $\dfrac{9}{10}$
$+ \dfrac{7}{10}$

4. $\dfrac{27}{16}$
$- \dfrac{7}{16}$

5. $\dfrac{15}{4}$
$- \dfrac{1}{4}$

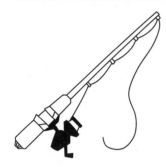

To add or subtract mixed numbers, first work with the fractions. Then work with the whole numbers.

$5\dfrac{2}{9}$
$+ 4\dfrac{1}{9}$

$9\dfrac{3}{9} = 9\dfrac{1}{3}$

$8\dfrac{6}{7}$
$- 3\dfrac{2}{7}$

$5\dfrac{4}{7}$

Add or subtract. Write each answer in lowest terms.

6. $2\dfrac{1}{7}$
$+ 3\dfrac{3}{7}$

7. $15\dfrac{7}{8}$
$- 8\dfrac{7}{8}$

8. $1\dfrac{5}{12}$
$+ 4\dfrac{5}{12}$

9. $17\dfrac{11}{15}$
$- 17\dfrac{8}{15}$

10. $47\dfrac{5}{6}$
$+ 26\dfrac{5}{6}$

11. $9\dfrac{5}{6}$
$- 6\dfrac{1}{6}$

12. $4\dfrac{7}{16}$
$+ 9\dfrac{3}{16}$

13. $3\dfrac{11}{12}$
$- 1\dfrac{5}{12}$

14. $1\dfrac{3}{5}$
$+ 6\dfrac{3}{5}$

15. $12\dfrac{9}{10}$
$- 9\dfrac{3}{10}$

16. $4\dfrac{4}{5}$
$- 3\dfrac{1}{5}$

17. $7\dfrac{3}{10}$
$+ 8\dfrac{3}{10}$

18. $11\dfrac{3}{4}$
$- 5\dfrac{1}{4}$

19. $16\dfrac{5}{8}$
$+ 5\dfrac{3}{8}$

20. $50\dfrac{5}{9}$
$- 24\dfrac{2}{9}$

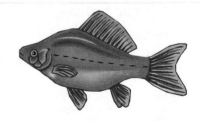

Adding and Subtracting Mixed Numbers with Like Denominators

Change fractions with unlike denominators to fractions with **like** denominators. Add the fractions. Then add the whole numbers.

Sometimes you must regroup the sum.

$$5\frac{1}{2} = 5\frac{3}{6}$$
$$+2\frac{2}{3} = 2\frac{4}{6}$$
$$7\frac{7}{6} = 8\frac{1}{6}$$

Add. Write each sum in lowest terms.

1. $1\frac{1}{2}$
    $+8\frac{1}{4}$

2. $5\frac{5}{6}$
    $+2\frac{1}{2}$

3. $6\frac{1}{3}$
    $+5\frac{1}{2}$

4. $1\frac{3}{4}$
    $+9\frac{1}{3}$

5. $3\frac{1}{4}$
    $+3\frac{6}{8}$

6. $2\frac{1}{8}$
    $+3\frac{3}{4}$

7. $6\frac{2}{3}$
    $+3\frac{5}{9}$

8. $7\frac{3}{4}$
    $+9\frac{1}{6}$

9. $8\frac{3}{10}$
    $+7\frac{4}{5}$

10. $5\frac{7}{8}$
    $+3\frac{5}{6}$

11. $27\frac{2}{3}$
    $+46\frac{5}{7}$

12. $62\frac{9}{10}$
    $+19\frac{1}{4}$

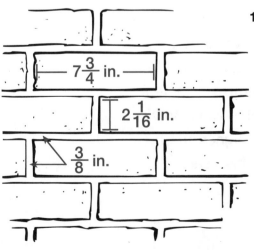

$7\frac{3}{4}$ in.

$2\frac{1}{16}$ in.

$\frac{3}{8}$ in.

13. What is the distance from the bottom of one brick to the bottom of the one above it?

14. What is the length of two bricks laid end to end and the mortar between them?

Change fractions with unlike denominators to fractions with like denominators. Subtract the fractions. Then subtract the whole numbers.

Sometimes you must regroup before you can subtract the fractions.

$$9\frac{1}{4} = 9\frac{1}{4} = 8\frac{5}{4}$$
$$-2\frac{1}{2} = 2\frac{2}{4} = 2\frac{2}{4}$$
$$\overline{\phantom{-2\frac{1}{2} = 2\frac{2}{4} = }6\frac{3}{4}}$$

Subtract. Write each difference in lowest terms.

1. $5\frac{2}{3}$
   $-1\frac{4}{9}$

2. $4\frac{3}{8}$
   $-1\frac{3}{4}$

3. $12\frac{1}{2}$
   $-7\frac{1}{7}$

4. $15\frac{3}{5}$
   $-7\frac{2}{3}$

5. 8
   $-2\frac{5}{8}$

6. $6\frac{7}{8}$
   $-3\frac{1}{2}$

7. $21\frac{2}{3}$
   $-8\frac{5}{6}$

8. $18\frac{3}{4}$
   $-9\frac{1}{3}$

9. $12\frac{1}{6}$
   $-3\frac{4}{9}$

10. 18
    $-7\frac{3}{5}$

11. $14\frac{2}{15}$
    $-6\frac{3}{5}$

12. $16\frac{1}{4}$
    $-9\frac{5}{6}$

13. Wesley jumped $2\frac{1}{2}$ meters in the long jump. Eileen jumped $1\frac{5}{8}$ meters. How much farther did Wesley jump than Eileen?

14. Last year, Wesley could jump over a pole $1\frac{1}{4}$ meters high. He can jump $1\frac{1}{3}$ meters high this year. How much higher can he jump this year?

Subtracting Mixed Numbers with Unlike Denominators

Read and solve each problem. Write the answer in lowest terms.

1. Sonja had $6\frac{1}{2}$ dozen red roses and $4\frac{1}{2}$ dozen yellow roses for sale. How many dozen roses did she have for sale?

2. Mr. Romanov brought 32 pounds of sausage to market. By noon, he had sold $27\frac{3}{4}$ pounds. How much sausage was left?

3. Ivan sold $25\frac{1}{4}$ pounds of sweet peppers and $6\frac{1}{8}$ pounds of chili peppers today. How many pounds of peppers did he sell in all?

4. Erin had $41\frac{3}{8}$ pounds of strawberries. She threw out $3\frac{7}{8}$ pounds of bad ones. How many pounds were left for sale?

5. Nick sold $72\frac{3}{10}$ pounds of flounder and $96\frac{7}{10}$ pounds of catfish. How many pounds of these fish did he sell in all?

6. Chika had $55\frac{1}{3}$ pounds of American cheese. By the end of the day, she had only $12\frac{3}{4}$ pounds left. How many pounds did she sell?

7. Celeste sold $20\frac{3}{4}$ dozen blueberry muffins and $27\frac{1}{3}$ dozen bran muffins. How many dozen muffins did she sell in all?

8. Nathan started the day with $38\frac{1}{6}$ pounds of beans. He sold all but $3\frac{1}{2}$ pounds. How many pounds did he sell?

Add or subtract. Write each answer in lowest terms.

1. $\dfrac{1}{4}$
    $+ \dfrac{3}{7}$

2. $5\dfrac{1}{3}$
    $- 2\dfrac{2}{3}$

3. $4\dfrac{3}{8}$
    $+ 2\dfrac{3}{8}$

4. $\dfrac{17}{24}$
    $+ \dfrac{1}{6}$

5. $2\dfrac{1}{12}$
    $- \dfrac{5}{6}$

6. $\dfrac{5}{16}$
    $+ \dfrac{7}{16}$

7. $6\dfrac{1}{3}$
    $+ 1\dfrac{4}{15}$

8. $3\dfrac{1}{6}$
    $- 2\dfrac{5}{8}$

9. $\dfrac{13}{18}$
    $- \dfrac{2}{9}$

10. $\dfrac{3}{4}$
    $+ \dfrac{3}{8}$

11. $3\dfrac{7}{20}$
    $- \dfrac{1}{4}$

12. $\dfrac{2}{3}$
    $- \dfrac{1}{2}$

13. $2\dfrac{1}{6}$
    $- 1\dfrac{5}{9}$

14. $1\dfrac{7}{24}$
    $+ 2\dfrac{14}{24}$

15. $4\dfrac{2}{5}$
    $- 1\dfrac{1}{2}$

16. $4\dfrac{3}{4}$
    $+ 3\dfrac{3}{5}$

17. Daria fed her dog $\dfrac{3}{4}$ pound of canned food and $1\dfrac{1}{3}$ pounds of dry food today. How much food was that in all?

18. Boris opened a 50-pound bag of puppy food. The puppies ate $10\dfrac{1}{5}$ pounds of it in two days. How much food was left in the bag?

Adding and Subtracting Fractions and Mixed Numbers—Practice

Multiply to find a fraction of a fraction.

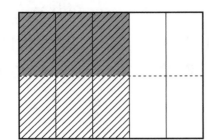

$\frac{3}{5}$ of the figure is lined.

$\frac{1}{2}$ of the lined part is shaded.

What part of the whole is lined and shaded?

$\frac{1}{2}$ of $\frac{3}{5}$ = $\frac{1}{2}$ × $\frac{3}{5}$ = $\frac{1 \times 3}{2 \times 5}$ = $\frac{3}{10}$

Multiply. Write each answer in lowest terms.

1. $\frac{1}{2} \times \frac{1}{3} =$

2. $\frac{3}{4} \times \frac{1}{2} =$

3. $\frac{2}{3} \times \frac{3}{4} =$

4. $\frac{1}{3} \times \frac{2}{5} =$

5. $\frac{1}{2} \times \frac{1}{4} =$

6. $\frac{1}{4} \times \frac{1}{3} =$

7. $\frac{5}{6} \times \frac{1}{2} =$

8. $\frac{1}{4} \times \frac{2}{5} =$

9. $\frac{2}{3} \times \frac{1}{2} =$

10. $\frac{3}{8} \times \frac{2}{3} =$

11. $\frac{3}{4} \times \frac{3}{4} =$

12. $\frac{7}{8} \times \frac{1}{4} =$

13. $\frac{1}{8} \times \frac{4}{5} =$

14. $\frac{1}{3} \times \frac{1}{9} =$

15. $\frac{6}{7} \times \frac{2}{3} =$

16. $\frac{3}{4} \times \frac{5}{6} =$

17. $\frac{5}{8} \times \frac{2}{5} =$

18. $\frac{1}{3} \times \frac{3}{4} =$

Solve.

19. Zareh had $\frac{1}{2}$ gallon of paint. She used $\frac{1}{2}$ of that amount to paint a chair. What part of a gallon did she use?

_____

20. Gavin had $\frac{5}{6}$ quart of brush cleaner. He used $\frac{2}{3}$ of it. What part of a quart did he use?

Multiply to find a fraction of a whole number.

First, change the whole number to a fraction. Then multiply. Write the product in lowest terms.

$\frac{1}{5}$ of 10 = $\frac{1}{5}$ × 10 $\frac{3}{4}$ of 8 = $\frac{3}{4}$ × 8

$\frac{1}{5}$ × $\frac{10}{1}$ = $\frac{10}{5}$ = 2 $\frac{3}{4}$ × $\frac{8}{1}$ = $\frac{24}{4}$ = 6

Multiply. Write each answer in lowest terms.

1. $\frac{1}{2}$ × 8 =

2. 9 × $\frac{1}{3}$ =

3. $\frac{1}{4}$ × 20 =

4. 9 × $\frac{2}{3}$ =

5. $\frac{1}{8}$ × 16 =

6. 12 × $\frac{5}{6}$ =

7. $\frac{3}{8}$ × 16 =

8. 36 × $\frac{2}{9}$ =

9. $\frac{1}{5}$ × 15 =

10. 12 × $\frac{3}{4}$ =

11. $\frac{4}{5}$ × 10 =

12. 24 × $\frac{1}{2}$ =

13. $\frac{1}{5}$ × 20 =

14. 14 × $\frac{2}{7}$ =

15. $\frac{2}{3}$ × 18 =

The Bergville Walkathon was 30 kilometers long. The table shows what fraction of the distance each person finished. Find how many kilometers each person walked.

Name	Fraction Walked	Total Kilometers
Ruby	$\frac{2}{3}$	$\frac{2}{3}$ of 30 =
Hank	$\frac{1}{2}$	
Sally	$\frac{9}{10}$	
Farid	$\frac{5}{6}$	
Diane	$\frac{4}{5}$	

Multiplying Fractions and Whole Numbers

To multiply mixed numbers, first change them to fractions greater than 1. Then multiply. Write the answer in lowest terms.

$$1\frac{1}{5} \times 2\frac{1}{2} = \frac{6}{5} \times \frac{5}{2} = \frac{30}{10} = 3$$

$$\frac{1}{3} \times 3\frac{2}{5} = \frac{1}{3} \times \frac{17}{5} = \frac{17}{15} = 1\frac{2}{15}$$

Multiply. Write each answer in lowest terms.

1. $2\frac{1}{3} \times 1\frac{1}{2} =$

2. $\frac{5}{6} \times 1\frac{1}{3} =$

3. $1\frac{2}{5} \times 1\frac{1}{4} =$

4. $2\frac{1}{2} \times 4 =$

5. $3\frac{2}{3} \times 4\frac{1}{2} =$

6. $1\frac{5}{6} \times 12 =$

7. $6\frac{4}{5} \times \frac{1}{7} =$

8. $\frac{1}{3} \times 2\frac{2}{3} =$

9. $3 \times 1\frac{2}{5} =$

10. $1\frac{1}{8} \times \frac{3}{4} =$

11. $1\frac{3}{5} \times 2\frac{1}{3} =$

12. $8 \times \frac{2}{3} =$

13. Ann spent $1\frac{1}{2}$ hours at the pool on each of 5 days. How much time did she spend there in all?

14. Luis had $1\frac{1}{4}$ pints of juice. He drank $\frac{5}{6}$ of that amount. How much did he drink?

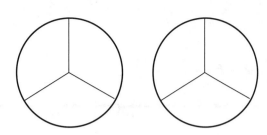

To find how many $\frac{1}{3}$s are in 2, divide.

$2 \div \frac{1}{3}$ is the same as 2×3, or 6.

Check the answer by multiplying.

$6 \times \frac{1}{3} = 2$

Use the pictures to help you divide.

1. $2 \div \frac{1}{2} = 2 \times 2 = 4$

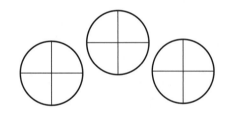

2. $3 \div \frac{1}{3} =$

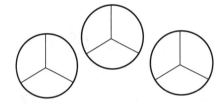

3. $4 \div \frac{1}{2} =$

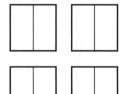

4. $3 \div \frac{1}{4} =$

5. $4 \div \frac{1}{3} =$

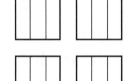

6. $2 \div \frac{1}{4} =$

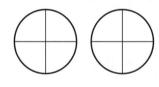

7. $4 \div \frac{1}{4} =$

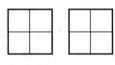

8. $1 \div \frac{1}{5} =$

9. $3 \div \frac{1}{2} =$

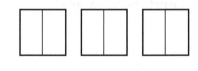

Solve.

10. A box contains 6 cups of cereal. If a serving is $\frac{1}{2}$ cup, how many servings are in the box?

11. A bag holds 8 cups of nuts. If a serving is $\frac{1}{3}$ cup, how many servings are in the bag?

Dividing Whole Numbers by Fractions

Read and solve each problem. Write the answer in lowest terms.

1. On her first try, Corina jumped $6\frac{1}{12}$ feet. The second time, she jumped $7\frac{5}{12}$ feet. How much farther did she jump the second time?

2. The swim team practiced $2\frac{1}{6}$ hours on Wednesday and $4\frac{1}{2}$ hours Saturday. How many hours did the team practice this week?

3. Rafael's team scored 28 points. Rafael scored $\frac{3}{4}$ of the points. How many points did he score?

4. Satori ran 5 miles on a track today. If the track is $\frac{1}{4}$ mile long, how many times did she run around the track?

5. Darwin ran for 3 hours this week. If he ran for $\frac{1}{2}$ hour at a time, how many times did he go running?

6. A football game lasted $3\frac{1}{2}$ hours. Mai could stay only $\frac{4}{5}$ of that time. How long did she stay?

7. Clyde ran $3\frac{1}{3}$ miles on Friday. On Saturday, he ran $4\frac{2}{7}$ times that distance. How far did Clyde run on Saturday?

8. Vivian can easily lift $10\frac{1}{2}$ pounds of weights. She wants to lift $2\frac{2}{3}$ times as many pounds. How many pounds does she want to lift?

Tenths, hundredths, and thousandths can be written as fractions or as decimals.

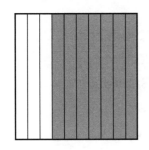 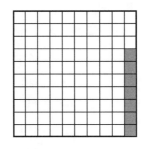 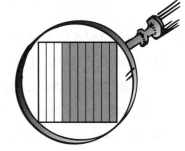

$$\frac{7}{10} = 0.7 \qquad \frac{7}{100} = 0.07 \qquad \frac{7}{1000} = 0.007$$

Write each fraction or mixed number as a decimal.

1. $\frac{3}{10}$ = _____

2. $\frac{29}{100}$ = _____

3. $9\frac{102}{1000}$ = _____

4. $7\frac{45}{100}$ = _____

5. $\frac{74}{1000}$ = _____

6. $35\frac{9}{100}$ = _____

7. $\frac{38}{100}$ = _____

8. $\frac{982}{1000}$ = _____

9. $28\frac{8}{1000}$ = _____

10. $4\frac{99}{100}$ = _____

11. $\frac{406}{1000}$ = _____

12. $100\frac{1}{10}$ = _____

Write a decimal for each number name.

13. 8 and 2 tenths _____

14. 5 tenths _____

15. 1 and 73 hundredths _____

16. 26 hundredths _____

17. 2 and 205 thousandths _____

18. 47 and 6 thousandths _____

19. 17 hundredths _____

20. 8 and 52 thousandths _____

21. 400 and 2 tenths _____

22. 621 thousandths _____

23. 19 and 4 hundredths _____

24. 180 and 123 thousandths _____

Decimals: Place Value

To compare decimals, compare the digits in the same places.

The digits in the ones and tenths places of both numbers are the same.

But 5 hundredths is less than 6 hundredths. So 2.556 is less than 2.562.

$2.556 < 2.562$

Compare each pair of decimals below. Write >, <, or =.

1. 2.3 ◯ 3.2

2. 8.5 ◯ 8.4

3. 4.30 ◯ 4.29

4. 1.609 ◯ 1.610

5. 7.01 ◯ 7.10

6. 9.21 ◯ 9.210

7. 23.4 ◯ 2.34

8. 4.57 ◯ 4.75

9. 0.398 ◯ 0.397

10. 0.45 ◯ 0.450

11. 0.886 ◯ 0.89

12. 0.91 ◯ 1.1

13. 16.42 ◯ 1.642

14. 0.17 ◯ 0.171

15. 6.29 ◯ 6.3

16. 92.8 ◯ 91.96

17. 3.007 ◯ 3.060

18. 5.09 ◯ 4.99

Listed below are ten cities in the United States and the amount of rain (in inches) each city received in a recent year. List the cities and rainfalls in order, beginning with the lowest rainfall.

YEARLY RAINFALL

City	Inches
Baltimore, MD	41.62
Boston, MA	41.55
Charleston, WV	43.66
Hartford, CT	43.00
Louisville, KY	42.94
New York, NY	43.56
Philadelphia, PA	41.18
Portland, ME	42.15
Richmond, VA	43.77
Wilmington, DE	43.63

_____

_____

_____

_____

_____

_____

_____

_____

_____

_____

Add decimals the same way you add whole numbers.

Add.

1. 16.75
    + 9.25
    ‾‾‾‾‾‾‾
    26.00

2. 0.58
    +0.14

3. 0.043
    +0.267

4. 8.6
    +3.9

5. 15.76
    +42.96

6. 109.1
    +199.7

7. 3.857
    +5.806

8. 62.78
    +15.04

9. 498.75
    +487.59

10. 562.16
    +108.63

11. 25.834
    +60.179

12. 37.095
    +19.963

13. 10.84
    32.56
    + 4.92

14. 376.8
    109.4
    +253.4

15. 8.042
    4.731
    +1.659

16. 61.504
    30.298
    +27.153

Solve. Remember to line up the decimal points.

17. Dr. Wong is working 0.783 kilometer north of the ship. Dr. Kamal is 0.898 kilometer directly south of the ship. How far apart are they?

18. Mud sample A is a tube 20.8 centimeters long. Mud sample B is 11.7 centimeters longer than A. How long is sample B?

19. Dr. Wong collected 13.72 kilograms of rocks on her first dive and 19.89 kilograms on the second dive. How much do her samples weigh in all?

20. The current at Cape Nom travels 3.55 kilometers an hour. At Zen Point, it moves 4.77 kilometers an hour faster. How fast does it move there?

Adding Decimals

Subtract decimals the same way you subtract whole numbers.

Subtract.

1. 12.98
    − 9.75
    ───────
    3.23

2. 9.6
    −4.9

3. 0.74
    −0.28

4. 0.243
    −0.065

5. 409.1
    −299.7

6. 8.306
    −6.357

7. 52.76
    −13.86

8. 6.140
    −3.942

9. 308.75
    −209.77

10. 70.153
    −69.294

11. 25.934
    − 8.976

12. 91.504
    −30.928

13. 4.052
    −2.386

14. 376.80
    −176.81

15. 60.01
    −40.32

16. 86.200
    − 6.345

Solve. Remember to line up the decimal points.

17. One trail to Gold Creek is 9.75 miles long. Another trail is 14.81 miles long. How much longer is the second trail than the first?

18. Kirsten's pack weighs 21.8 pounds. Graham's pack weighs 24.3 pounds. How much heavier is Graham's pack?

19. During the day, the temperature rose to 78.8°F. At night, it fell to 45.9°F. How many degrees did the temperature drop?

20. Kirsten found 0.013 ounce of gold in the creek. Graham found 0.006 ounce. How much more gold did Kirsten find than Graham?

Subtracting Decimals

To add or subtract decimals with different numbers of places, be careful to line them up on the decimal points. You can write zeros to help you.

```
  4.35        9.750
+ 0.20      - 2.125
  4.55        7.625
```

Rewrite each problem in vertical form. Then solve.

1. 52.6 + 18.43 =

2. 63.51 – 14.7 =

3. 8.472 + 0.9 =

4. 92.3 – 82.64 =

5. 405 – 27.9 =

6. 73.4 + 629 =

7. 16.01 + 8.592 =

8. 32.4 – 29.685 =

9. 8.4 + 25.76 =

10. 32.09 – 14.8 =

11. 65.12 – 8.234 =

12. 29.7 + 6.85 + 3.6 =

Solve. Remember to line up the decimal points.

13. Cassandra has 3 meters of canvas. If she uses 1.25 meters of it to stretch over a frame for a painting, how much will be left?

14. Chad's sculpture weighs 23.5 kilograms. He welds a piece that weighs 3.74 kilograms onto it. How much does it weigh now?

Adding and Subtracting Decimals

Read and solve each problem. Be sure to check your answer.

1. One turkey weighs 16.04 pounds. A second turkey weighs 18.7 pounds. How much more does the heavier turkey weigh?

2. Kayla mixed 1.419 quarts of cranberry juice and 3.785 quarts of apple juice. How many quarts of cranberry-apple punch did she make?

3. Malcolm's turkey should be roasted for 4.5 hours. It has been in the oven 1.7 hours. How much longer must it roast?

4. Melia peeled 4.8 pounds of potatoes. Tara peeled 2.64 pounds. How many pounds of potatoes did they peel together?

5. Drew had 1.67 pounds of carrots. After trimming them, he had 1.5 pounds left. How much did he trim off?

6. A bag of sugar weighed 4.97 pounds. Then Sarah used 0.675 pound to make a pumpkin pie. How much sugar was left in the bag?

7. The Sanchezs' turkey weighed 18.4 pounds. After dinner, only 4.79 pounds of bones were left. How much meat had there been?

8. Pete poured 0.75 quart of milk into the soup. Later, he added 0.46 quart more milk. How much milk did he put in the soup in all?

Multiplying decimals is like multiplying whole numbers.

0.5	0.5	0.05
×3	×0.3	×0.3
1.5	0.15	0.015

The number of decimal places in the product is equal to the sum of the number of decimal places in the factors.

Place the decimal point correctly in each product.

1.   3.2
    ×1.8
    576

2.   10.6
    ×0.54
    5724

3.   8.9
    ×4
    356

4.   23.7
    ×0.16
    3792

5.   5.2
    ×8.4
    4368

Multiply.

6.   6.9
    ×5

7.   4.08
    ×0.3

8.   1.7
    ×0.6

9.   94
    ×0.8

10.   8.6
    ×0.02

11.   2.5
    ×19

12.   0.48
    ×7.3

13.   6.2
    ×0.45

14.   56
    ×9.2

15.   9.01
    ×6.8

16. A rat found its way through 1.36 meters of a maze. The entire maze is 6 times longer. How long is the entire maze?

17. A bag of rat food holds 3.75 kilograms. There are 2.5 bags of food in the supply closet. How much food is in the closet?

18. The average lab rat weighs 0.425 kilogram. If there are 15 rats in the lab, how much do they weigh altogether?

To multiply a decimal by—

       10, move the decimal point **one** place to the right. $10 \times 2.35 = 23.5$

       100, move the decimal point **two** places to the right. $100 \times 2.35 = 235.0$

       1,000, move the decimal point **three** places to the right. $1{,}000 \times 2.35 = 2{,}350.0$

Write zeros in the product if you need them to place the decimal point.

Multiply.

1. $10 \times 6.32 = $ _____

2. $100 \times 7.47 = $ _____

3. $5.03 \times 10 = $ _____

4. $100 \times 0.549 = $ _____

5. $1.904 \times 100 = $ _____

6. $200.86 \times 10 = $ _____

7. $0.875 \times 10 = $ _____

8. $0.036 \times 1{,}000 = $ _____

9. $1{,}000 \times 6.988 = $ _____

10. $10 \times 0.031 = $ _____

11. $9.7 \times 1{,}000 = $ _____

12. $357.992 \times 100 = $ _____

To divide a decimal by—

       10, move the decimal point **one** place to the left. $2.35 \div 10 = 0.235$

       100, move the decimal point **two** places to the left. $2.35 \div 100 = 0.0235$

       1,000, move the decimal point **three** places to the left. $2.35 \div 1{,}000 = 0.00235$

Write zeros in the quotient if you need them to place the decimal point.

Divide.

13. $6.58 \div 10 = $ _____

14. $7{,}925.1 \div 1{,}000 = $ _____

15. $371.57 \div 100 = $ _____

16. $529.6 \div 10 = $ _____

17. $153.225 \div 1{,}000 = $ _____

18. $4.6 \div 100 = $ _____

19. $27.84 \div 100 = $ _____

20. $0.415 \div 10 = $ _____

21. $28.9 \div 1{,}000 = $ _____

22. $8.324 \div 100 = $ _____

23. $90.525 \div 10 = $ _____

24. $1.78 \div 1{,}000 = $ _____

Dividing decimals is like dividing whole numbers.

$$
\begin{array}{r}
3.2 \\
6\,\overline{)\,19.2} \\
\underline{18} \\
1.2 \\
\underline{1.2}
\end{array}
\qquad
\begin{array}{r}
0.24 \\
14\,\overline{)\,3.36} \\
\underline{2\,8} \\
56 \\
\underline{56}
\end{array}
\qquad
\begin{array}{r}
0.05 \\
7\,\overline{)\,0.35} \\
\underline{35}
\end{array}
$$

When a decimal is divided by a whole number, the decimal point is placed in the quotient directly above its original position.

Place the decimal point correctly in each quotient.

1.
$$
\begin{array}{r}
8\;6 \\
8\,\overline{)\,68.8}
\end{array}
$$

2.
$$
\begin{array}{r}
9\;2 \\
33\,\overline{)\,303.6}
\end{array}
$$

3.
$$
\begin{array}{r}
0\;76 \\
21\,\overline{)\,15.96}
\end{array}
$$

4.
$$
\begin{array}{r}
0\;029 \\
5\,\overline{)\,0.145}
\end{array}
$$

Divide. Remember to place zeros in the quotient where necessary.

5. $4\,\overline{)\,3.84}$

6. $9\,\overline{)\,15.3}$

7. $3\,\overline{)\,0.168}$

8. $8\,\overline{)\,0.072}$

9. $26\,\overline{)\,33.8}$

10. $15\,\overline{)\,0.525}$

11. $78\,\overline{)\,2.262}$

12. $92\,\overline{)\,7.36}$

13. Ms. Atkinson sold 13.25 acres of land. If it was divided into 5 equal-sized parts, how big was each part?

14. A bag of candy weighs 2.88 pounds. If it holds 32 pieces of the same size, how much does each piece weigh?

15. In 7 days, a total of 5.95 inches of rain fell. What was the average amount of rain that fell per day?

Dividing Decimals

1. Fidel unloaded 45 boxes of floor tiles from a truck. Each box weighed 10.65 pounds. How many pounds of tiles did Fidel unload?

2. Mrs. Santos bought a pipe 9.5 feet long. She needed only 8.76 feet to make a repair. How much pipe did she have left?

3. Mr. Hayes bought a bag of 1,000 nails. If one nail weighed 0.004 pound, how much did the bag of nails weigh?

4. Rosanne emptied a box of 75 bolts into a bin at the hardware store. If the entire box weighed 3.75 pounds, how much did one bolt weigh?

5. Ms. Fitz bought three pieces of metal stovepipe that were 6.25, 4.5, and 2.6 feet long. How many feet of stovepipe did she buy?

6. Eduardo bought 52.5 feet of boards. If he got 7 boards of the same length, how long was each board?

7. Ms. Gerke bought 9 stair treads. They made a stack 11.25 inches high. How thick was each stair tread?

8. To make a repair, Scott needs 7 pieces of wood siding, each 1.75 feet long. How many feet does he need in all? Will one 8-foot length of siding be enough?

60 seconds = 1 minute
60 minutes = 1 hour
24 hours = 1 day
7 days = 1 week
365 days = 1 year
12 months = 1 year
100 years = 1 century

Use the table above to help you find the answer to each problem.

1. San Pablo was founded 4 centuries ago. How many years ago was it founded?

2. Consuelo is sick. Her doctor says this kind of sickness lasts only 72 hours. How many days is that?

3. Ishmael can husk an ear of corn in 12 seconds. How many ears of corn can he husk in 1 minute?

4. Mr. Harlan subscribes to a monthly magazine. Because he never throws out any, 72 issues have piled up. How many years has he subscribed to it?

5. Professor Morgan spent 9 weeks this summer digging for fossils. How many days did she spend digging?

6. The Yees watched a movie that lasted 132 minutes. How many hours and minutes did it last?

7. A clock was guaranteed for 2 years. It worked for 697 days. How much time was left on the guarantee?

8. Dr. Zelinsky conducted an experiment that lasted 3 years, 7 weeks, and 2 days. How many days did it last?

Problem Solving: Using Units of Time

Solve each problem. Write A.M. or P.M. when the answer is a time of day. Remember, A.M. is used with times from midnight to noon, and P.M. is used with times from noon to midnight.

1. The trip to Washington, D.C., takes 6 hours and 15 minutes. The Watsons have been traveling 3 hours and 45 minutes. How much longer will the trip last?

6 h 15 min
−3 h 45 min

(Think: 5h 75 min)

2. A bus tour of Washington leaves the hotel at 9:00 A.M. It lasts 2 hours and 15 minutes. What time is it over?

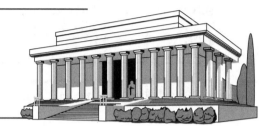

3. The Watsons spent 2 hours and 20 minutes at the Air and Space Museum and 3 hours and 15 minutes at the National Gallery. How much time did they spend in all?

4. The Watsons entered the White House at 10:30 A.M. They left 1 hour and 30 minutes later. What time did they leave?

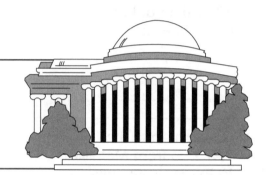

5. The Watsons spent 1 hour and 50 minutes at the Library of Congress. If they left it at 4:30 P.M., what time had they arrived?

6. A play at the Kennedy Center starts at 8:00 P.M. It is 6:18 P.M. now. How much time does the family have until the play starts?

7. On Tuesday, the Watsons arrived at the National Zoo at 10:05 A.M. They left at 2:39 P.M. How much time did they spend there?

8. The train arrived at the Watsons' home town at 10:40 P.M. If the trip took 6 hours and 15 minutes, what time did the train leave Washington, D.C.?

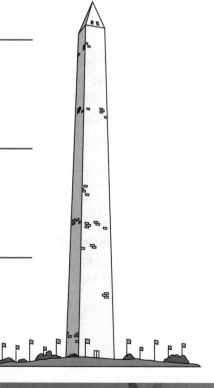

Problem Solving: Finding Elapsed Time

79

Morning Buses from Beachside to Pratt Falls					
Beachside	Meffville	Artburg	San Lobo	Exton	Pratt Falls
6:10	6:22	6:28	6:32	6:40	6:55
7:05	7:17	7:23	7:27	7:35	7:50
7:35	7:47	7:53	7:57	8:05	8:20
8:10	8:22	8:28	8:32	8:40	8:55
8:45	8:57	9:03	9:07	9:15	9:30
9:30	9:42	9:48	9:52	10:00	10:15
10:25	10:37	10:43	10:47	10:55	11:10
11:05	11:17	11:23	11:27	11:35	11:50

Use the schedule to solve each problem.

1. Felipe caught the 7:05 bus in Beachside. What time did he arrive in Pratt Falls?

2. Carrie has a dentist appointment in Pratt Falls at 8:30. What time should she catch the bus in San Lobo?

3. Giovanni took the 7:47 bus from Meffville to Exton. How long did his trip take?

4. Xiao Ling wants to get to Artburg as close to 10:00 as she can. What time should she leave Beachside?

5. Alison boarded the bus in Artburg at 10:43. What time will she arrive in Pratt Falls?

6. Ken got off the bus at 8:32 in San Lobo. What time had he boarded the bus in Beachside?

7. Trina took the 6:10 bus from Beachside to Pratt Falls. How long did the trip take?

8. Brett arrived in Exton at 7:35. He got on the bus in Artburg. How long did the trip take?

Problem Solving: Using a Schedule

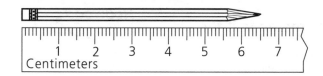

A **millimeter** (mm) is $\frac{1}{10}$, or 0.1, of a **centimeter** (cm).

The pencil is 65 millimeters, or 6.5 centimeters, long.

10 millimeters = 1 centimeter

Complete.

1. 7 cm = _____ mm

2. 50 mm = _____ cm

3. 9.6 cm = _____ mm

4. 0.3 cm = _____ mm

5. 10 mm = _____ cm

6. 16.4 cm = _____ mm

7. 5 mm = _____ cm

8. 19 mm = _____ cm

9. 100 mm = _____ cm

10. 0.2 cm = _____ mm

11. 4.5 cm = _____ mm

12. 852 mm = _____ cm

Measure each object. Give its length in millimeters and centimeters.

13. _____ mm
_____ cm
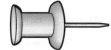

14. _____ mm
_____ cm

15. _____ mm _____ cm

16. _____ mm
_____ cm

17. _____ mm
_____ cm

18. _____ mm _____ cm

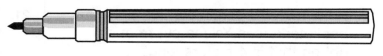

19. _____ mm _____ cm

20. _____ mm _____ cm

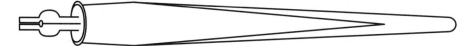

21. _____ mm _____ cm

Measurement: Millimeter and Centimeter

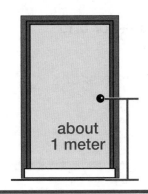

about 1 meter

The **meter** (m) is the basic metric unit for measuring length.

100 centimeters = 1 meter

The **kilometer** (km) is used for measuring long distances.

1,000 meters = 1 kilometer

Redwood

12 kilometers

★ *CAPITAL CITY*

Complete.

1. 200 centimeters = _____ meters

2. 150 centimeters = _____ meters

3. 6.5 meters = _____ centimeters

4. 5 kilometers = _____ meters

5. 1.68 meters = _____ centimeters

6. 3.25 kilometers = _____ meters

7. 3 meters = _____ centimeters

8. 8,000 meters = _____ kilometers

9. 725 centimeters = _____ meters

10. 4,500 meters = _____ kilometers

11. 2.5 kilometers = _____ meters

12. 2,650 meters = _____ kilometers

Write *centimeters, meters,* or *kilometers* to complete each sentence.

13. Ten-year old Tina is 138 _____ tall.

14. The distance from New York City to Philadelphia is 149 _____.

15. Lee, our basketball star, is nearly 2 _____ tall.

16. In a few minutes, Nora had swum the 300 _____ across the lake.

17. That old car has been driven over 250,000 _____.

18. I need a frame for a photograph that measures 7.6 by 12.7 _____.

19. Victor gasped as 50 or 60 _____ of fishing line disappeared.

Solve.

20. How many 10-centimeter-long bookmarks can Yelena cut from a ribbon that is 4 meters long?

21. How many kilometers can Armando walk in an hour if he walks at the rate of 80 meters per minute?

The **milliliter** (mL) and **liter** (L) are metric units of capacity.

about
1 milliliter

 about
1 liter

1,000 milliliters = **1** liter

Circle the best answer for the capacity of each item.

1. an eyedropper	1 mL	1 L	4. a picnic cooler	4 L 40 L
2. a bucket	10 mL	10 L	5. a bathtub	10 L 100 L
3. a juice glass	10 mL	100 mL	6. a test tube	6 mL 6 L

Complete.

7. 2 liters = _____ milliliters

8. 3,000 milliliters = _____ liters

9. 1.5 liters = _____ milliliters

10. 5,600 milliliters = _____ liters

11. 9.8 liters = _____ milliliters

12. 500 milliliters = _____ liter

The **milligram** (mg), **gram** (g), and **kilogram** (kg) are metric units of mass.

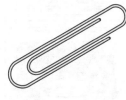
about
1 gram

about
1 kilogram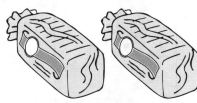

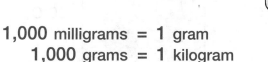
1,000 milligrams = **1** gram
1,000 grams = **1** kilogram

Circle the best answer for the mass of each item.

13. a bean	1 mg	1 g	16. a grain of salt	1 mg 1,000 mg
14. a pair of shoes	1 g	1 kg	17. a football player	50 kg 100 kg
15. a small dog	10 kg	100 kg	18. a slice of bread	25 g 250 g

Complete.

19. 5 kilograms = _____ grams

20. 7,000 milligrams = _____ grams

21. 1.5 kilograms = _____ grams

22. 1.8 grams = _____ milligrams

23. 3.2 kilograms = _____ grams

24. 700 grams = _____ kilogram

The degree Celsius (°C) is a unit for measuring temperature in the metric system.

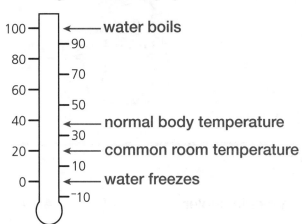

Write the degrees Celsius for the following:

1. normal body temperature _____

2. freezing point of water _____

3. common room temperature _____

4. boiling point of water _____

Circle the best temperature for each scene.

5.
   40°C
   80°C
   100°C

6.
   50°C
   100°C
   200°C

7.
   ⁻5°C
   15°C
   30°C

8.
   ⁻10°C
   10°C
   60°C

9.
   35°C
   60°C
   90°C

10.
   50°C
   180°C
   350°C

Shade each thermometer to show the given outdoor temperature. Then circle the word that best describes that temperature.

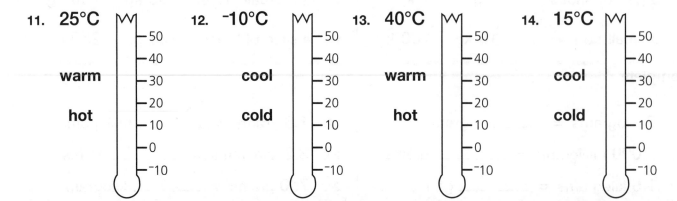

11. **25°C**   warm   hot

12. **⁻10°C**   cool   cold

13. **40°C**   warm   hot

14. **15°C**   cool   cold

Measurement: Degrees Celsius

Some problems contain hidden information.

Deena opened a 2-liter jug of milk. She used 750 milliliters of it. How much milk was left in the jug?

You know that 1 liter equals 1,000 milliliters. So 2 liters equal 2,000 milliliters.

Now subtract.

$$\begin{array}{r} 2,000 \\ -\ \ \ 750 \\ \hline 1,250 \end{array}\text{ milliliters}$$

Read and solve each problem below. Be careful—some problems have more than one step.

1. For exercise, Dae-Ho runs 4.5 kilometers a day on an indoor track that is 750 meters long. How many times does he run around the track?

2. Michelle drinks 8 glasses of water a day. Each glass holds 240 milliliters. How many liters and milliliters of water does Michelle drink each day?

3. A teenager needs 1.2 grams of calcium a day. A glass of milk contains 288 milligrams. How many glasses provide enough calcium for one day?

4. One type of fast-food burger contains 1.5 grams of salt. This is 5 times as much as a person needs a day. How many milligrams are needed?

5. A kilogram of ground beef makes 8 burgers. If one burger contains 25 grams of protein, how many grams of a burger are not protein?

6. A vitamin tablet has 18 milligrams of iron. If a person took one a day, how many grams of iron would he or she get in a year?

7. A liter of juice drink contains only 120 milliliters of actual fruit juice. How many milliliters are not fruit juice?

8. In January, Emilio was 1.61 meters tall. He grew 3 centimeters. How many centimeters tall is he now?

On the right is a picture of a credit card. Use an inch ruler to find the —

1. length to the nearest inch   _____ in.

2. width to the nearest inch   _____

3. length to the nearest $\frac{1}{2}$ inch   _____

4. width to the nearest $\frac{1}{8}$ inch   _____

5. length to the nearest $\frac{1}{8}$ inch   _____

SUPER CARD

1 234 56789 10 1112

J R SMITH   EXPIRES 10/15

Below are the outlines of a dollar bill and some coins. Measure the —

6. length of the bill to the nearest $\frac{1}{16}$ inch _____

7. width of the bill to the nearest $\frac{1}{16}$ inch _____

8. diameter of the penny to the nearest $\frac{1}{4}$ inch _____

9. diameter of the nickel to the nearest $\frac{1}{16}$ inch _____

10. diameter of the quarter to the nearest $\frac{1}{16}$ inch _____

Draw lines with the following lengths.

11. $3\frac{5}{8}$ inches

12. $6\frac{3}{16}$ inches

13. $4\frac{1}{2}$ inches

14. $1\frac{15}{16}$ inches

15. $3\frac{3}{4}$ inches

16. $2\frac{7}{8}$ inches

Measurement: Fractions of an Inch

$$12 \text{ inches} = 1 \text{ foot (ft)}$$
$$3 \text{ feet} = 1 \text{ yard (yd)}$$
$$36 \text{ inches} = 1 \text{ yard}$$
$$5{,}280 \text{ feet} = 1 \text{ mile (mi)}$$
$$1{,}760 \text{ yards} = 1 \text{ mile}$$

Complete.

1. 5 feet = _____ inches

2. 4 yards = _____ feet

3. 3 yards = _____ inches

4. 2 miles = _____ feet

5. 48 inches = _____ feet

6. $\frac{1}{2}$ mile = _____ yards

7. 6 feet and 8 inches = _____ inches

8. 47 yards = _____ feet

9. 12 yards and 1 foot = _____ feet

10. 120 inches = _____ feet

11. 1 mile and 240 yards = _____ yards

12. 180 inches = _____ yards

13. 30 inches = _____ feet and _____ inches

14. 26 feet = _____ yards and _____ feet

15. 10,000 feet = _____ mile and _____ feet

Solve. Be careful. Some problems may have more than one step.

16. Harvey bought two boards to build some shelves. One is 7 feet 8 inches long, and the other is 7 feet 10 inches long. What is their total length?

17. Greta has two pieces of cloth. One piece is 3 yards 1 foot long and the other is 2 yards 2 feet long. How much cloth did Greta buy in all?

18. Mrs. Tate is 5 feet 3 inches tall. Her daughter is 4 feet 8 inches tall. How much taller is Mrs. Tate?

19. Allen bought 2 yards of ribbon. He used 2 feet 9 inches of ribbon on each of two banners. How much ribbon does he have left?

Complete.

2 cups = 1 pint (pt)
2 pints = 1 quart (qt)
4 quarts = 1 gallon (gal)

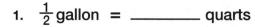

1. $\frac{1}{2}$ gallon = _____ quarts

2. 10 gallons = _____ quarts

3. $3\frac{1}{2}$ quarts = _____ pints

4. 1 gallon = _____ pints

5. 2 quarts = _____ cups

6. 18 pints = _____ gallons and _____ quart

7. 20 cups = _____ pints or _____ quarts

Complete.

16 ounces (oz) = 1 pound (lb)
2,000 pounds = 1 ton

8. $\frac{1}{4}$ pound = _____ ounces

9. 8 ounces = _____ pound

10. 22 ounces = _____ pound and _____ ounces

11. $3\frac{1}{2}$ pounds = _____ ounces

12. 70 ounces = _____ pounds and _____ ounces

13. $4\frac{1}{2}$ tons = _____ pounds

14. 12,000 pounds = _____ tons

Solve. Be careful. Some problems may have more than one step.

15. Mrs. Spivak had 5 gallons of gas. She used 1 gallon in her tractor and 3 quarts in her lawn mower. How much gas was left?

16. Ross sold 36 boxes of band candy. Each box weighs 12 ounces. What is the total weight in pounds of the candy Ross sold?

17. A 2-pound box of detergent sells for $4.80. A 48-ounce box sells for $5.76. Which package is the better buy?

18. A gallon jug of milk sells for $3.88. A quart sells for $1.54. How much money can Yana save by buying a gallon of milk in a gallon jug rather than by quarts?

Measurement: Customary Units of Capacity and Weight

Serves 8 people.　　　　　　5-Way Chili

Sauce:　$1\frac{1}{2}$ C chopped onions

$2\frac{1}{2}$ lb ground beef

one 14-oz can tomato sauce
3 C beef broth
4 T chili powder

$1\frac{1}{4}$ lb spaghetti, cooked

Toppings:　12 oz shredded cheese
one 15-oz can kidney beans
$\frac{3}{4}$ C chopped onions

Directions:　1. Brown the onions and the meat. Pour off the fat.
2. Add the tomato sauce, broth, and chili powder. Cook for 1 hour.
3. To serve "5-way," ladle sauce over spaghetti. Top with cheese, beans, and onions.

Use the information in the recipe to help you solve each problem. Check your answers.

1. Onions are used in both the sauce and as a topping. How many cups of onions does Earl need to make one recipe of chili?

2. Olivia has 3 pounds of ground beef. If she makes one recipe of chili, how many ounces of meat will she have left?

3. Naoko wants to make enough chili for 16 people. How much meat will he need?

4. How many pounds and ounces of cheese should Faith shred to make the recipe for 12 people?

5. How many quarts of broth will Clayton need to make the recipe for 32 people?

6. Robyn wants to make the recipe for only 4 people. How much meat should she use?

7. Kelsey has a 1-lb 6-oz can of kidney beans. If she uses the amount called for in the recipe, how many ounces will she have left?

8. If Jared makes one recipe, how many ounces of spaghetti would each person get if it is shared equally?

Some problems can be solved by making a table.

For every cup of sugar Joey uses in a recipe, he uses 1.5 cups of flour. If he uses 4 cups of sugar, how much flour will he need?

sugar	1	2	3	4
flour	1.5	3.0	4.5	6.0

He needs 6 cups of flour.

Make a table to find the answer to each problem.

1. Mrs. Havarro edits every 5 pages of her first draft into 2 pages of a final draft. If her first draft of a story was 25 pages long, how long was the final draft?

_____

2. There are 3 commercials during every 15 minutes of a program. If the program is 60 minutes long, how many commercials does it have?

_____

3. In Wellsville, the sun shines an average of 4 days out of every 7. How many sunny days could be expected in a month of 28 days?

_____

4. Colin makes 3 baskets for every 5 shots he takes. How many baskets can he expect to make if he takes 20 shots?

_____

5. The grocery store sells 2 cans of tomatoes for $0.99. How much would 10 cans cost?

_____

6. For every 2 sandwiches, the Deli Shop uses 0.5 pound of meat. How many pounds will the shop use to make 12 sandwiches?

Problem Solving: Making a Table

A **ratio** is a way to compare two numbers.

There are 3 girls and 1 boy in Devon's family.

The ratio of girls to boys is 3 to 1, or $\frac{3}{1}$.

The ratio of boys to girls is 1 to 3, or $\frac{1}{3}$.

The ratio of girls to children in the family is 3 to 4, or $\frac{3}{4}$.

The ratio of boys to children in the family is 1 to 4, or $\frac{1}{4}$.

Write each ratio two ways.

  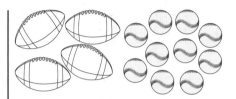

1. apples to bananas

    _____

2. bananas to apples

    _____

3. bananas to fruit

    _____

4. dogs to cats

    _____

5. cats to dogs

    _____

6. cats to pets

    _____

7. baseballs to footballs

    _____

8. footballs to baseballs

    _____

9. balls to baseballs

    _____

10. There are 3 stores and 2 houses.

    stores to houses _____

    houses to buildings _____

11. There are 5 guppies and 4 zebra fish.

    zebra fish to guppies _____

    fish to zebra fish _____

12. There are 6 rings and 6 bracelets.

    bracelets to rings _____

    rings to bracelets _____

13. There are 2 hammers and 6 wrenches.

    wrenches to hammers _____

    hammers to tools _____

14. There are 10 magazines and 5 books.

    books to magazines _____

    magazines to books _____

15. There are 8 tulips and 24 daisies.

    tulips to daisies _____

    daisies to flowers _____

Two ratios are equal if they can be written as equivalent fractions.

Shirley uses 2 bananas and 3 apples to make fruit salad. She wants to make 3 times as much with the same ratio of bananas to apples. What is an equal ratio to 2 to 3?

$\frac{2}{3} = \frac{2 \times 3}{3 \times 3} = \frac{6}{9}$, so $\frac{2}{3}$ and $\frac{6}{9}$ are **equal ratios**.

Decide if the ratios are equal. Write = or ≠ (does not equal) in each circle.

1. $\frac{3}{4}$ ◯ $\frac{9}{12}$

2. $\frac{2}{5}$ ◯ $\frac{6}{15}$

3. $\frac{2}{3}$ ◯ $\frac{4}{7}$

4. $\frac{7}{8}$ ◯ $\frac{24}{32}$

5. $\frac{4}{9}$ ◯ $\frac{12}{27}$

6. $\frac{5}{3}$ ◯ $\frac{30}{18}$

7. $\frac{5}{6}$ ◯ $\frac{40}{48}$

8. $\frac{3}{10}$ ◯ $\frac{6}{30}$

9. $\frac{1}{8}$ ◯ $\frac{8}{100}$

10. $\frac{3}{1}$ ◯ $\frac{12}{5}$

11. $\frac{5}{4}$ ◯ $\frac{20}{16}$

12. $\frac{4}{5}$ ◯ $\frac{20}{25}$

Write the missing number in each pair of equal ratios.

13. $\frac{1}{2} = \frac{}{10}$

14. $\frac{3}{4} = \frac{9}{}$

15. $\frac{5}{3} = \frac{}{9}$

16. $\frac{2}{5} = \frac{10}{}$

17. $\frac{4}{2} = \frac{2}{}$

18. $\frac{8}{12} = \frac{}{3}$

19. $\frac{4}{8} = \frac{1}{}$

20. $\frac{6}{9} = \frac{}{36}$

21. $\frac{24}{} = \frac{3}{2}$

22. $\frac{}{24} = \frac{4}{6}$

23. $\frac{50}{40} = \frac{}{8}$

24. $\frac{3}{} = \frac{1}{9}$

Use equal ratios to solve each problem.

25. To make tuna salad, Noah uses 1 can of tuna and 2 stalks of celery. How much celery does he need for 4 cans?

26. Lucinda uses 2 eggs to make 24 cupcakes. If she wants to make 48 cupcakes, how many eggs does she need?

Equal Ratios

A **scale drawing** shows something larger or smaller than actual size. A **scale** tells the ratio of the drawing size to the actual size.

EAST SIDE MALL

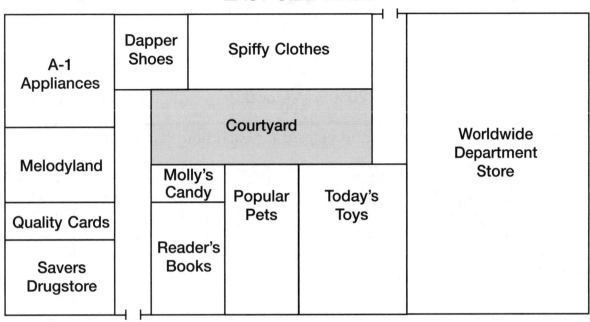

Scale: 1 cm = 4 m

Use the scale drawing and your centimeter ruler to find the actual length and width of each store or area of the mall.

	Length	Width
1. Worldwide Department Store	_____	_____
2. Today's Toys	_____	_____
3. Popular Pets	_____	_____
4. Quality Cards	_____	_____
5. Dapper Shoes	_____	_____
6. Reader's Books	_____	_____
7. Molly's Candy	_____	_____
8. A-1 Appliances	_____	_____
9. Courtyard (shaded area only)	_____	_____
10. Savers Drugstore	_____	_____
11. Spiffy Clothes	_____	_____
12. Melodyland	_____	_____

You can show hundredths as a fraction, a decimal, or a **percent**.

100% equals 100 hundredths: $\frac{100}{100}$ or 1

$75\% = \frac{75}{100}$ or 0.75 $20\% = \frac{20}{100}$ or 0.2 $5\% = \frac{5}{100}$ or 0.05

Write the correct fraction, decimal, and percent for each figure or set below.

Fraction with denominator of 100	$\frac{75}{100}$				
Decimal	0.75				
Percent	75%				

Write each decimal as a fraction and as a percent.

1. 0.64 =   2. 0.9 =   3. 0.42 =

4. 0.38 =   5. 0.06 =   6. 0.26 =

Write each fraction as an equivalent fraction with a denominator of 100 and as a percent.

7. $\frac{3}{4}$ =   8. $\frac{4}{10}$ =   9. $\frac{1}{2}$ =

10. $\frac{5}{20}$ =   11. $\frac{7}{10}$ =   12. $\frac{3}{5}$ =

Write each percent as a decimal and as a fraction.

13. 32% =   14. 8% =   15. 74% =

16. 19% =   17. 50% =   18. 7% =

Introduction to Percent

There are 120 members in the caving club. At least once a month, 75% of them go on a trip. How many members is that?

To find a percent of a number, follow these steps.
First, write the percent as a decimal.

75% = 0.75

Then multiply.

$$\begin{array}{r} 120 \\ \times 0.75 \\ \hline 90.00 \end{array}$$

90 members go on trips.

Find the percent of each number.

1. 10% of 480

2. 50% of 700

3. 25% of 80

4. 5% of 300

5. 80% of 640

6. 30% of 270

7. 45% of 960

8. 96% of 200

9. 7% of 1,200

Solve.

10. A cave is 750 meters deep. Yakov has gone down to 60% of this depth. How many meters has he gone down?

11. Only 5% of the 120 caving club members have explored the Winding Way Cave. How many people is that?

There are 20 people in the chorus. This week, 6 of them missed rehearsal because they had sore throats. What percent of the chorus missed rehearsal?

To find what percent 6 is of 20, follow these steps.

First, write a fraction for the ratio.

Next, divide the numerator by the denominator.

Finally, write the quotient as a percent.

6 of $20 = \dfrac{6}{20}$

$$20\overline{)6.00} \quad 0.30$$

$0.30 = 30\%$

30% of the chorus missed rehearsal.

Find what percent the first number is of the second.

1. **5** sopranos
   10 singers

2. **8** cats
   25 pets

3. **2** chocolate cookies
   8 cookies

4. **1** canoe
   5 boats

5. **9** mysteries
   30 books

6. **4** red cars
   40 cars

7. **3** rattlesnakes
   60 snakes

8. **9** broken cups
   12 cups

9. **6** diamonds
   24 jewels

Solve.

10. The chorus has 18 songs to learn for the spring concert. So far, they have learned 9 of them. What percent have they learned?

11. A rehearsal lasts 45 minutes. The chorus spent 27 minutes on one song today. What percent of their rehearsal time was spent on that song?

Finding a Percent

Some problems can be solved by finding a percent of a number or by finding what percent one number is of another.

At Ritz Books, a paperback costs $5.00. At Super Discount Books, the same book costs 20% less. How much less does the book cost?

Find 20% of $5.00.

$$\begin{array}{r} \$5.00 \\ \times\,0.20 \\ \hline \$1.0000 \end{array}$$

The book costs $1.00 less.

Solve.

1. A sweatshirt that usually costs $20 is now $5 off. What percent of the usual price is the discount?

2. Gisa's lunch cost $9.50. She wants to leave a tip of 18%. How much should she leave?

3. Matt put $500 in a savings account. It earns 8% interest in a year. How much money does the account earn in a year?

4. A CD player is priced at $80. At the end of the year, its price is reduced to $60. What percent of the original price is the sale price?

5. The Mendozas' rent is $500 a month. On January 1, it will go up 10%. How much will the increase be?

6. A puppy was listed for sale at $50. Cindy convinced the owner to sell the puppy to her for $35. What percent of the asking price did Cindy pay?

7. A DVD costs $15.00. Sales tax is 5% of the price. How much is the sales tax?

8. Lionel earns $10.50 an hour. He gets a raise of 4%. How much more is he now earning?

A **line** is a straight path with no endpoints. It is named by any two points on it.

A **ray** is half a line. It has one endpoint. The endpoint is always named first.

A **line segment** is part of a line. It has two endpoints. Either one can be named first.

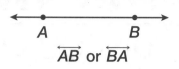

$\overleftrightarrow{AB}$ or $\overleftrightarrow{BA}$

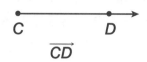

$\overrightarrow{CD}$

$\overline{EF}$ or $\overline{FE}$

Name each line, line segment, and ray below. Cross out any figure that is not a line, line segment, or ray.

1.

_____

2.

_____

3.

_____

4.

_____

5.

_____

6.

_____

7.

_____

8.

_____

9.

_____

10.

_____

Decode the message below by drawing each line, ray, and line segment listed in the box.

| $\overline{GH}$ | $\overrightarrow{WF}$ | $\overleftrightarrow{AQ}$ | $\overline{IJ}$ | $\overrightarrow{UE}$ | $\overline{GY}$ | $\overline{YZ}$ | $\overline{UV}$ | $\overline{CK}$ | $\overrightarrow{WX}$ | $\overrightarrow{ST}$ | $\overline{HZ}$ | $\overline{KL}$ | $\overrightarrow{RB}$ | $\overline{SK}$ | $\overrightarrow{CD}$ |

A   B   C   D   E   F   G   H

I   J   K   L   M   N   O   P

Q   R   S   T   U   V   W   X   Y   Z

Geometry: Basic Concepts

An **angle** is formed by two rays with the same endpoint. The rays are the sides of the angle. The endpoint is the vertex.

An angle is named by three points. The vertex is always the middle letter.

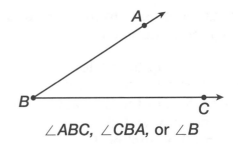

∠ABC, ∠CBA, or ∠B

Name each angle three ways.

1.

_____

2.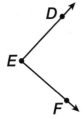

_____

3.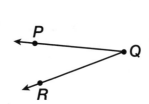

_____

4.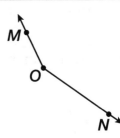

_____

Angles are measured in degrees (°).

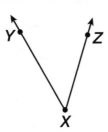

A right angle measures 90°.

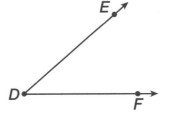

An acute angle measures less than 90°.

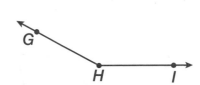

An obtuse angle measures more than 90°.

Write *acute, right,* or *obtuse* to describe each angle.

5.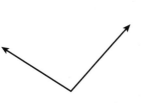

_____

6.

_____

7.

_____

8.

_____

9.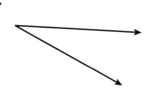

_____

10.

_____

11.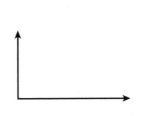

_____

12.

_____

A protractor is used to measure angles. It is marked in degrees.

To use it, line up the vertex of the angle with the mark at the center bottom of the protractor. Line up one ray with 0°. Then read the number the other ray points to.

This angle measures 105°.

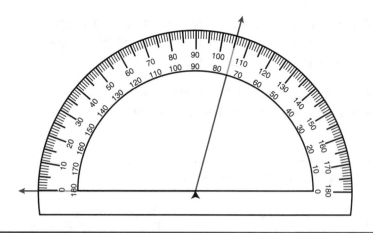

Use a protractor to measure each angle. Write the measure inside the angle.

1.

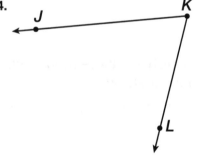

2.

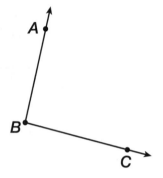

3.

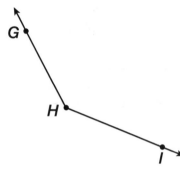

4.

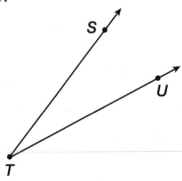

5.

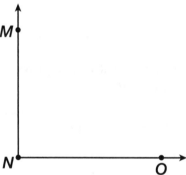

6.

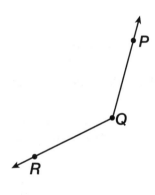

7.

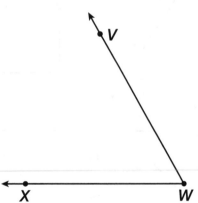

8.

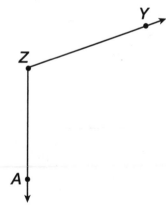

9.

Geometry: Measuring Angles

Parallel lines never meet. They are always the same distance apart.

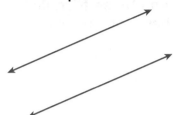

Intersecting lines meet. They form angles.

Perpendicular lines are intersecting lines that form right angles.

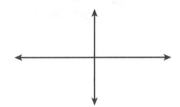

Rays and line segments can also be parallel or intersecting.

Use the figure below to complete the following.

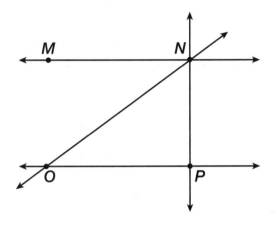

1. Name two parallel lines. _____

2. Name two intersecting lines that are not perpendicular. _____

3. Name two perpendicular lines.

   _____

4. Name a line that is perpendicular to $\overleftrightarrow{MN}$.

   _____

5. Name two angles formed by intersecting lines.

   _____

Draw the following figures.

6. $\overleftrightarrow{AB}$ parallel to $\overleftrightarrow{CD}$

7. $\overleftrightarrow{EF}$ perpendicular to $\overleftrightarrow{GH}$

8. $\overleftrightarrow{RS}$ parallel to $\overleftrightarrow{TU}$ and $\overleftrightarrow{RT}$ perpendicular to $\overleftrightarrow{TU}$

A triangle is a polygon with three sides and three angles. The sum of the angles is always 180°. Triangles are named for the kinds of angles or the number of equal sides they have.

A right triangle has 1 right angle.

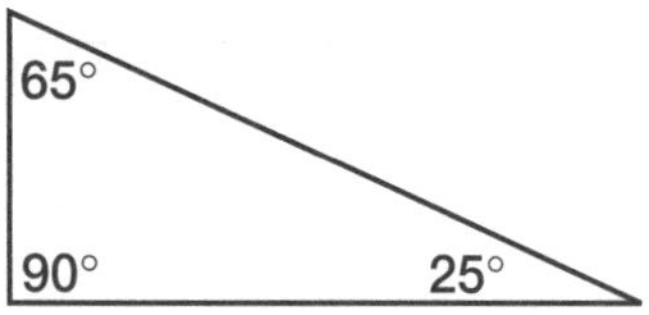

65°
90° 25°

An acute triangle has 3 acute angles.

40°
70° 70°

An obtuse triangle has 1 obtuse angle.

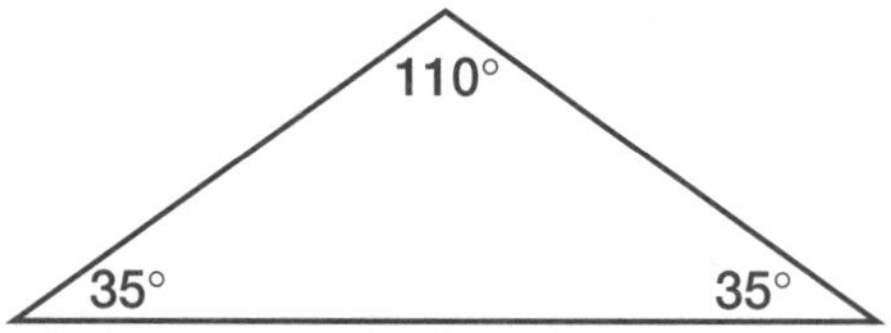

110°
35° 35°

An equilateral triangle has 3 equal sides.

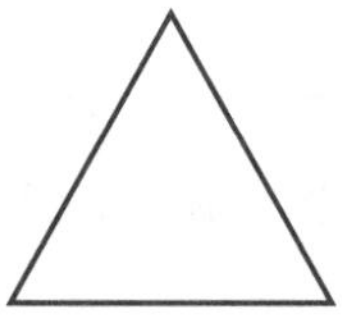

An isosceles triangle has 2 equal sides.

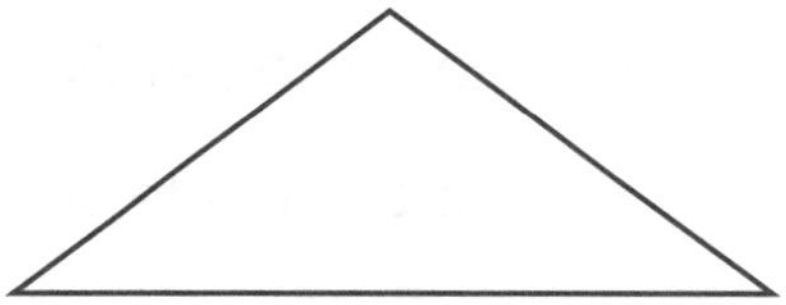

A scalene triangle has no equal sides.

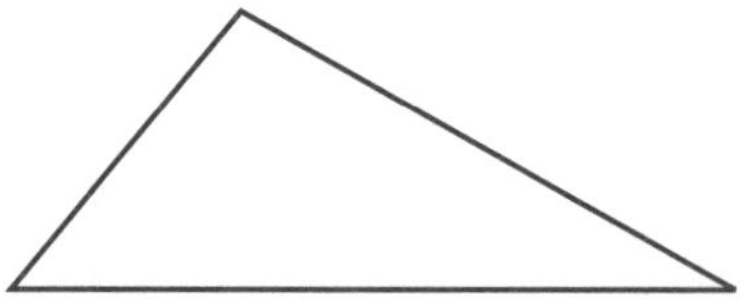

Write *right, acute,* or *obtuse* to describe each triangle.

1.

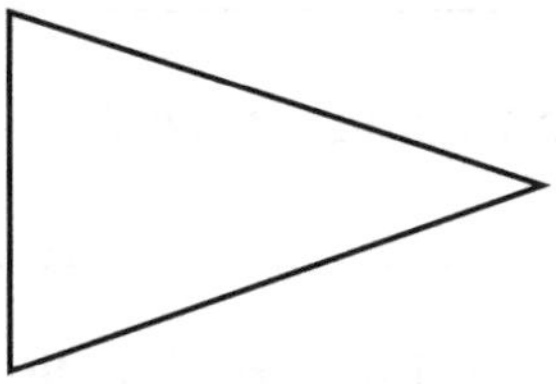

_____

2.

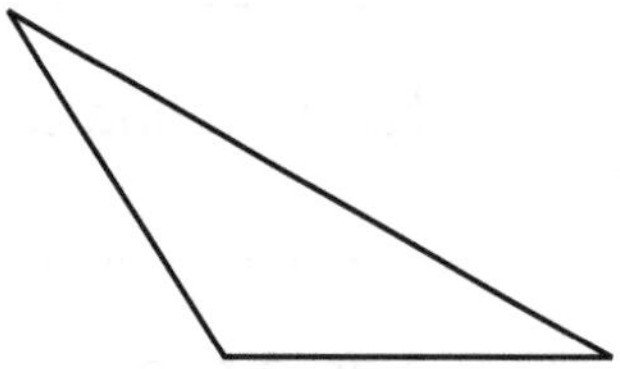

_____

3.

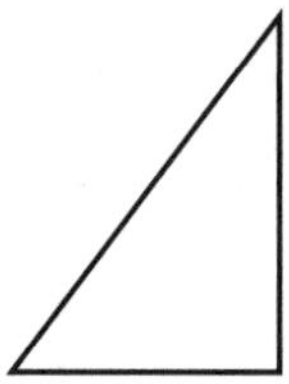

_____

Write *equilateral, isosceles,* or *scalene* to describe each triangle.

4.

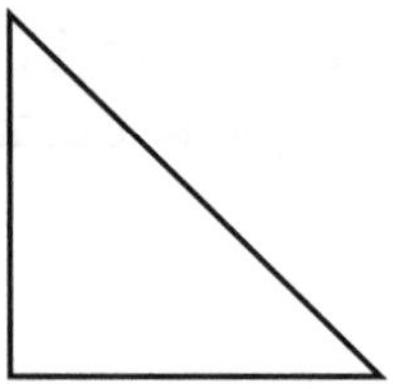

_____

5.

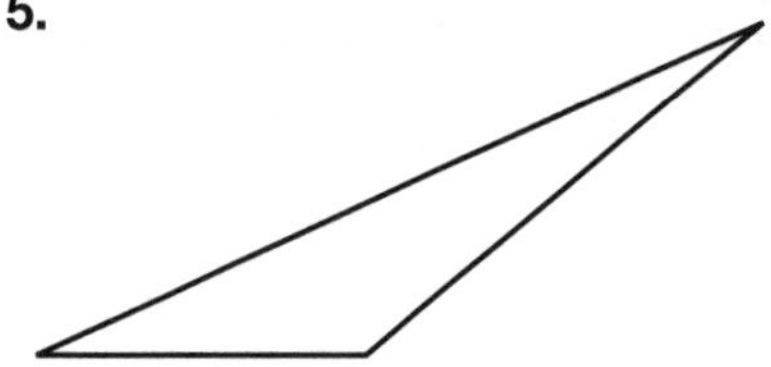

_____

6.

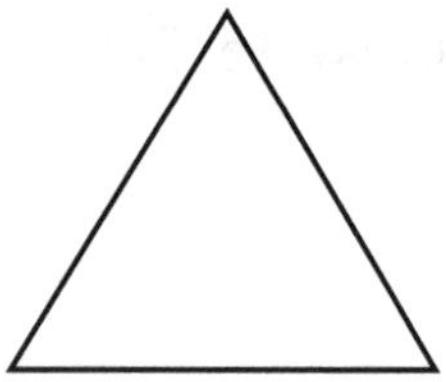

_____

Find the measure of the third angle.

7.

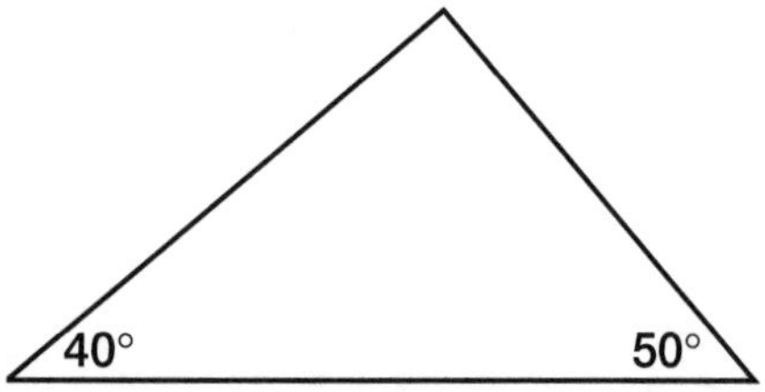

40°   50°

8.

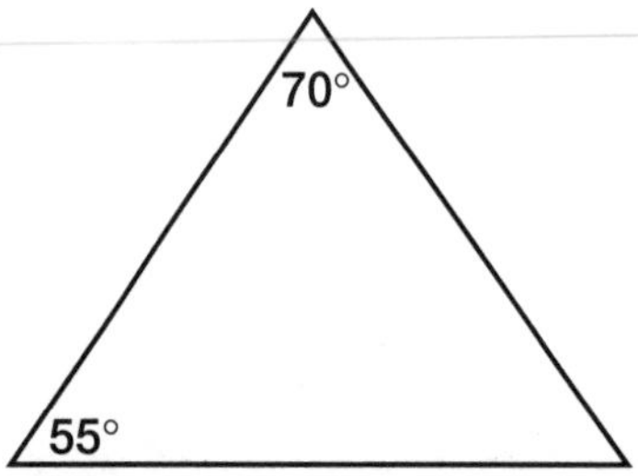

70°
55°

9.

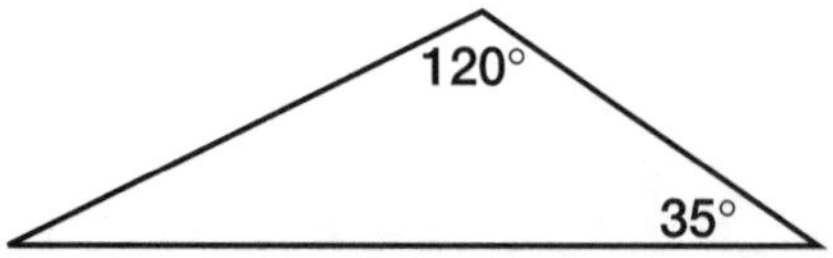

120°
35°

Geometry: Triangles

A quadrilateral is a polygon with four sides. Some kinds of quadrilaterals have special names.

A **parallelogram** has opposite sides that are parallel and the same length.

A **rhombus** is a kind of parallelogram. All four sides are the same length.

A **rectangle** is a parallelogram with four right angles.

A **square** is a kind of rectangle. All four sides are the same length.

Use the figures above to answer the following questions.

1. Which side is parallel to $\overline{AB}$ on the parallelogram? _____

2. Which side is the same length as $\overline{BD}$ on the parallelogram? _____

3. Is $\overline{EF}$ parallel to $\overline{EG}$ on the rhombus? _____

4. Which side or sides are the same length as $\overline{FH}$ on the rhombus? _____

5. Which angles are 90° on the rectangle? _____

6. Which sides are the same length on the square? _____

Write *parallelogram, rhombus, rectangle,* or *square* to describe each figure.

7.

_____

8.

_____

9.

_____

10.

_____

11.

_____

12.

_____

13.

_____

14.

_____

Congruent polygons are the same size and shape. The corresponding sides are the same length, and the corresponding angles are equal.

Similar polygons are the same shape but may be different sizes. The corresponding angles are equal, but the corresponding sides may be different lengths.

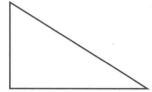 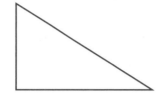 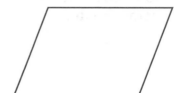 

Complete.

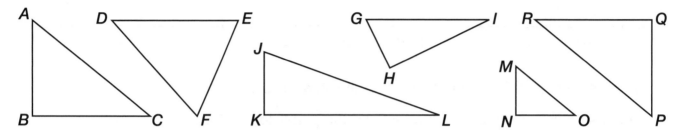

1. The triangle that is congruent to △*ABC* is _____ .

2. The corresponding sides of the congruent triangles are $\overline{AB}$ and _____, $\overline{BC}$ and _____, and $\overline{CA}$ and _____.

3. The corresponding angles of the congruent triangles are ∠*A* and _____,

   ∠*B* and _____, and ∠*C* and _____.

4. A triangle that is similar but not congruent to △*ABC* is _____ .

5. The corresponding angles of △*ABC* and the similar triangle are ∠*A* and _____,

   ∠*B* and _____, and ∠*C* and _____.

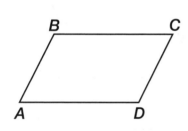 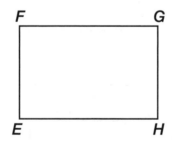 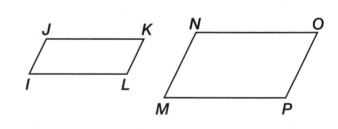

6. The figure that is congruent to quadrilateral *ABCD* is _____ .

7. The corresponding sides of the congruent quadrilaterals are $\overline{AB}$ and _____, $\overline{BC}$ and

   _____, $\overline{CD}$ and _____, and $\overline{DA}$ and _____.

8. The corresponding angles of the congruent quadrilaterals are ∠*A* and _____,

   ∠*B* and _____, ∠*C* and _____, and ∠*D* and _____.

Geometry: Congruent and Similar Polygons

A **symmetrical** figure can be folded along a line of symmetry. The two parts exactly fit each other.

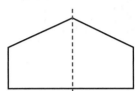

Some figures have more than one line of symmetry

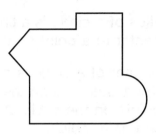

Other figures have no lines of symmetry.

Draw at least one line of symmetry through each figure.

1.

2.

3.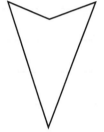

4.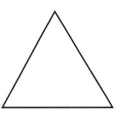

5.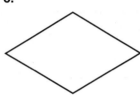

6.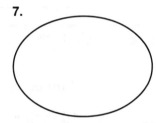

7.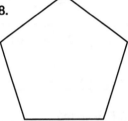

8.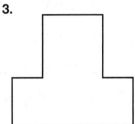

Complete each figure so the dashed line is a line of symmetry.

9.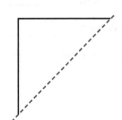

10.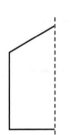

11.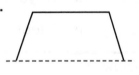

12.

13.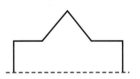

14.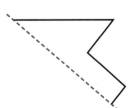

15.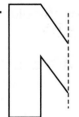

16.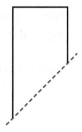

A circle is a closed figure. All points on a circle are the same distance from the center.

A radius of a circle is a line segment from the center to a point on the circle.

A diameter of a circle is a line segment which passes through the center and has endpoints on the circle. A diameter is twice as long as a radius.

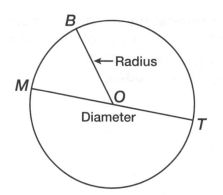

Use the circle below to answer each question.

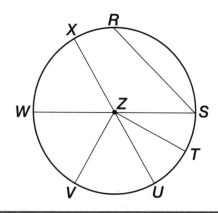

1. What point is the center of the circle? _____

2. What are two diameters of it? _____

3. What are six radii? _____

4. Is $\overline{RS}$ a diameter of the circle? _____

5. Why or why not? _____

_____

How long is the diameter of a circle if the radius is—

6. 7 feet? _____

7. 2 miles? _____

8. 15 inches? _____

9. 3.5 yards? _____

10. 10 inches? _____

11. 8.6 feet? _____

How long is the radius of a circle if the diameter is—

12. 10 miles? _____

13. 18 yards? _____

14. 36 inches? _____

15. 1 foot? _____

16. 9 feet? _____

17. 7 inches? _____

Follow the instructions below.

Trace the circle on the right.

Label the center A.

Draw two diameters that are perpendicular to each other. Label them $\overline{BC}$ and $\overline{DE}$.

Draw three radii. Label them $\overline{AF}$, $\overline{AG}$, and $\overline{AH}$.

Geometry: Circles

The **perimeter** (*P*) of a figure is the distance around it. One way to find perimeter is by adding the lengths of the sides.

To find the perimeter of a square or rectangle, multiply.

$P = 4 \times length$
$P = 4 \times 2$
$P = 8$ cm

$P = (2 \times length) + (2 \times width)$
$P = (2 \times 5) + (2 \times 1)$
$P = 12$ cm

Add to find the perimeter of each figure.

1.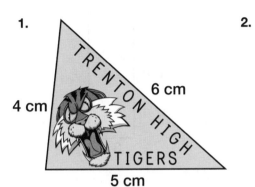

4 cm   6 cm
5 cm

$P =$ _____ cm

2.

2 ft
2 ft   2 ft
2 ft   2 ft
2 ft

$P =$ _____ ft

3.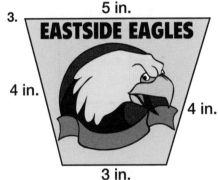

5 in.
4 in.   4 in.
3 in.

$P =$ _____ in.

Multiply to find the perimeter of each square or rectangle.

4.

15 ft

$P =$ _____ ft

5.

8 cm
10 cm

$P =$ _____ cm

6.

6 yd
18 yd

$P =$ _____ yd

7. a rectangle; *l* = 22 m, *w* = 7 m

$P =$ _____ m

8. a square; *l* = 25 in.

$P =$ _____ in.

9. a rectangle; *l* = 100 cm, *w* = 50 cm

$P =$ _____ cm

10. a square; *l* = 3 in.

$P =$ _____ in.

11. a rectangle; *l* = 9 ft, *w* = 2 ft

$P =$ _____ ft

12. a square; *l* = 2 km

$P =$ _____ km

The **area** (*A*) of a figure is the number of square units inside it. One way to find area is to count the square units.

To find the area of a square or rectangle, multiply the length times the width.

Remember to write area in square units, such as in.² or cm².

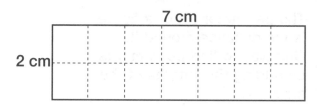

7 cm

2 cm

$A = length \times width$

$A = 7 \times 2$

$A = 14$ cm²

Multiply to find the area of each figure.

1.

2 cm

$A =$ _____ cm²

2.

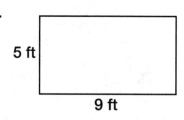

5 ft

9 ft

$A =$ _____ ft²

3.

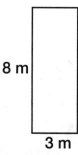

8 m

3 m

$A =$ _____ m²

4.

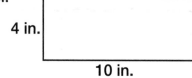

4 in.

10 in.

$A =$ _____ in.²

5.

6 km

$A =$ _____ km²

6.

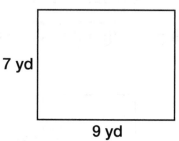

7 yd

9 yd

$A =$ _____ yd²

7. a square; *l* = 20 ft

$A =$ _____ ft²

8. a rectangle; *l* = 15 cm, *w* = 10 cm

$A =$ _____ cm²

9. a square; *l* = 9 mi

$A =$ _____ mi²

10. a rectangle; *l* = 50 m, *w* = 2 m

$A =$ _____ m²

11. a square; *l* = 100 ft

$A =$ _____ ft²

12. a rectangle; *l* = 15 in., *w* = 5 in.

$A =$ _____ in.²

Geometry: Area

The base of the triangle is the same as the length of the rectangle.

The height of the triangle is the same as the width of the rectangle.

The area of the triangle is half the area of the rectangle.

Remember to write area in square units.

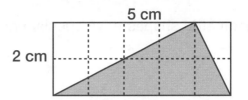

$A = \frac{1}{2} \times$ base $\times$ height

$A = \frac{1}{2} \times 5 \times 2$

$A = 5 \text{ cm}^2$

Multiply to find the area of each triangle.

1.

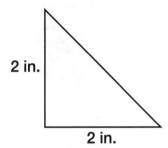

2 in.

2 in.

$A =$ _____ in.^{2}

2.

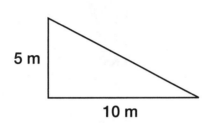

5 m

10 m

$A =$ _____ m^2

3.

5 ft

8 ft

$A =$ _____ ft^2

4.

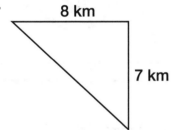

8 km

7 km

$A =$ _____ km^2

5.

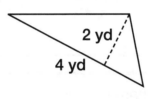

2 yd

4 yd

$A =$ _____ yd^2

6.

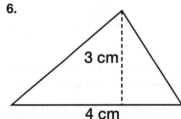

3 cm

4 cm

$A =$ _____ cm^2

7. $b = 8 \text{ mi}, h = 8 \text{ mi}$

8. $b = 20 \text{ cm}, h = 5 \text{ cm}$

9. $b = 25 \text{ m}, h = 10 \text{ m}$

$A =$ _____ mi^2

$A =$ _____ cm^2

$A =$ _____ m^2

10. $b = 7 \text{ km}, h = 12 \text{ km}$

11. $b = 12 \text{ ft}, h = 10 \text{ ft}$

12. $b = 30 \text{ m}, h = 20 \text{ m}$

$A =$ _____ km^2

$A =$ _____ ft^2

$A =$ _____ m^2

Geometry: Area of Triangles

109

Solid geometric shapes have special names.

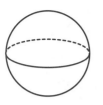 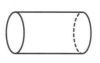 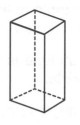 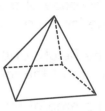

| sphere | cone | cylinder | cube | rectangular prism | square pyramid |

Name the shape of each numbered object in the picture below.

1.

_____

2.

_____

3.

_____

4.

_____

5.

_____

6.

_____

The parts of some solids have special names.

←Face

←Edge

←Vertex

Look at this triangular pyramid.
The flat surfaces are faces.
The faces meet at edges.
The edges meet at vertices.

Write the number of faces, edges, and vertices each shape has.

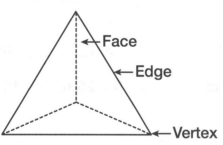

faces					
edges					
vertices					

Geometry: Solid Figures

The **volume** (V) of a solid figure is the number of cubic units inside it.

To find the volume of a rectangular solid, multiply the length times the width times the height.

Remember to write the volume in cubic units, such as in.³ or cm³.

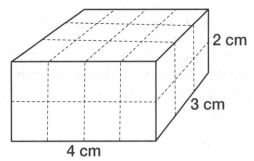

$V = length \times width \times height$

$V = 4 \times 3 \times 2$

$V = 24$ cm³

Find the volume of each rectangular solid.

1.

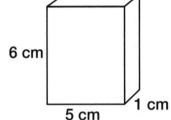

6 cm

5 cm   1 cm

V = _____ cm³

2.

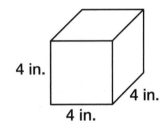

4 in.

4 in.

4 in.

V = _____ in.³

3.

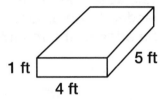

1 ft   5 ft

4 ft

V = _____ ft³

4.

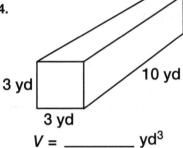

3 yd   10 yd

3 yd

V = _____ yd³

5.

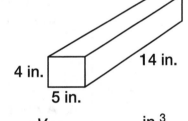

4 in.   14 in.

5 in.

V = _____ in.³

6.

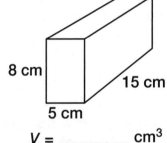

8 cm   15 cm

5 cm

V = _____ cm³

7. $l = 7$ ft, $w = 5$ ft, $h = 3$ ft

V = _____ ft³

8. $l = 2$ cm, $w = 2$ cm, $h = 4$ cm

V = _____ cm³

9. $l = 4$ yd, $w = 3$ yd, $h = 3$ yd

V = _____ yd³

10. $l = 15$ in., $w = 5$ in., $h = 10$ in.

V = _____ in.³

11. $l = 5$ m, $w = 10$ m, $h = 3$ m

V = _____ m³

12. $l = 6$ ft, $w = 4$ ft, $h = 3$ ft

V = _____ ft³

Geometry: Volume

111

Drawing a picture can help you solve some problems.

When it is folded, Nadia's travel clock is 8 centimeters long, 6 centimeters wide, and 4 centimeters high. How much space does it take up then?

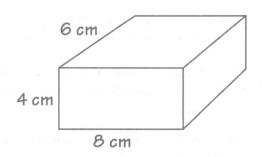

$$V = 8 \times 6 \times 4 = 192 \text{ cm}^3$$

Draw a picture to help you solve each problem.

1. The square ceiling of a room is 4 yards long on each side. How many yards of wallpaper border are needed to go around the edge of the room?

2. A carpet is 8 feet long and 6 feet wide. What is the area of the carpet?

3. A storage shed is 5 meters long, 4 meters wide, and 3 meters high. What is the volume of the shed?

4. A fence around the park swimming pool is 100 meters long and 58 meters wide. What is the total length of the fence?

5. A window is a triangle with a base of 3 feet and a height of 5 feet. What is the area of the window?

6. A briefcase is 18 inches long, 14 inches wide, and 3 inches deep. What is its volume?

7. A box is 20 centimeters long, 20 centimeters wide, and 20 centimeters high. What is the volume of the box?

8. A stage is a rectangle that is 28 yards long and 12 yards wide. What is its area?

An **ordered pair** of numbers, or coordinates, names the location of a point on a grid. The first number tells how many units to the right the point is. The second number tells how many units up the point is. For example, (5, 3) names a point that is 5 units to the right and 3 units up.

Name the ordered pair for each star.

1. A _____

2. B _____

3. C _____

4. D _____

5. E _____

6. F _____

7. G _____

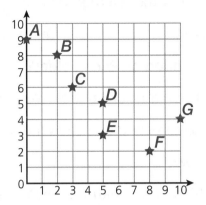

Name the point for each ordered pair.

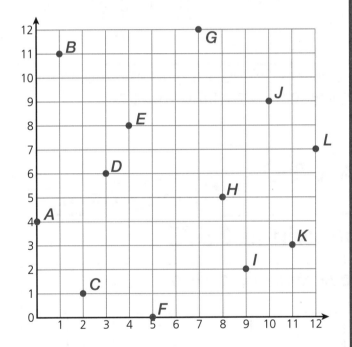

8. (12, 7) _____

9. (1, 11) _____

10. (8, 5) _____

11. (3, 6) _____

12. (10, 9) _____

13. (0, 4) _____

14. (7, 12) _____

15. (2, 1) _____

16. (11, 3) _____

17. (9, 2) _____

18. (4, 8) _____

19. (5, 0) _____

Graph and label the points below. Then draw the line segments.

A (0, 6)   B (5, 10)   C (10, 6)
D (8, 0)   E (2, 0)
$\overline{AC}$ $\overline{AD}$ $\overline{BD}$ $\overline{BE}$ $\overline{EC}$

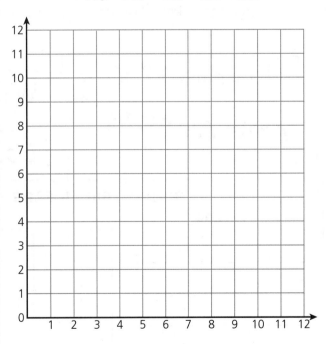

Geometry: Ordered Pairs

113

Tanisha is planning a January vacation. Use this bar graph to answer the questions.

1. What does this graph compare? _____

   _____

2. What is the average daily January temperature in

   Paris? _____ In Quebec City? _____

3. Is London or Paris colder? _____

4. Is New York or London warmer? _____

5. Water freezes at 32°F. Where is there likely to be

   snow? _____

6. Which is the warmest place Tanisha can go?

   _____

7. Which is the coldest place Tanisha can go?

   _____

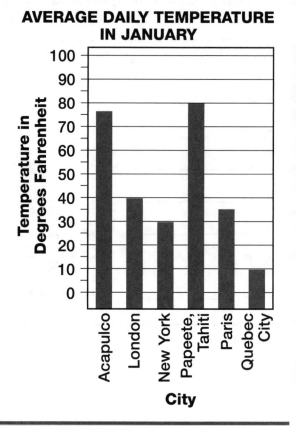

AVERAGE DAILY TEMPERATURE IN JANUARY

Tanisha decided to go to Acapulco, Mexico. She checked several airlines' Web sites to find the best price for tickets. Use her notes to complete this horizontal bar graph.

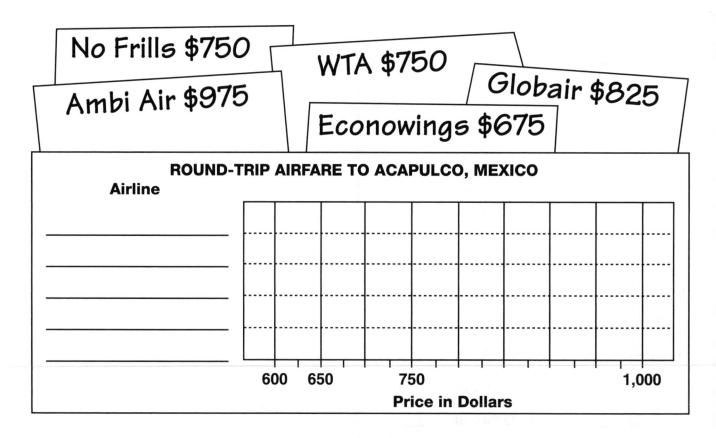

No Frills $750

WTA $750

Ambi Air $975

Globair $825

Econowings $675

ROUND-TRIP AIRFARE TO ACAPULCO, MEXICO

Airline

Price in Dollars

Use the line graph to answer the questions.

NORTHFIELD PARK USE

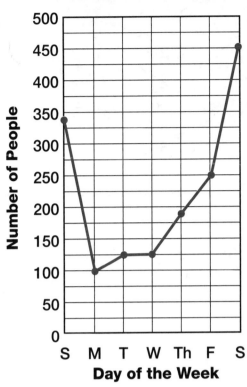

1. On which day did the most people use the park?

   _____ How many used it? _____

2. On which day did the fewest people use it?

   _____ How many used it? _____

3. On which days did the same number of people

   use it? _____

4. Did more than 200 people use the park on

   Thursday? _____ On Sunday? _____

5. How many people used the park on Friday?

   _____ On Sunday? _____

6. What is the difference between the greatest

   and the smallest number of users? _____

Use the information in the table to complete the line graph.

Year	Population
1900	4,500
1910	5,100
1920	6,400
1930	7,200
1940	7,500
1950	7,900
1960	8,300
1970	8,000
1980	7,500
1990	7,800
2000	8,100

POPULATION OF WINDERVILLE, 1900–2000

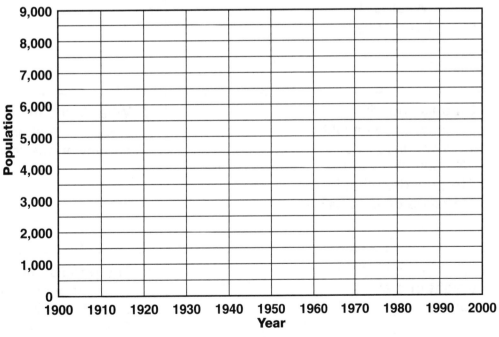

To find the **range** of a set of data, subtract the lowest number from the highest.

$$100 - 85 = 15$$

To find the **mean,** or average, add the numbers and divide by the number of items.

$$100 + 95 + 90 + 85 + 85 = 455$$
$$455 \div 5 = 91$$

To find the median, first put the numbers in order. Then find the number in the middle.

85   85   **90**   95   100

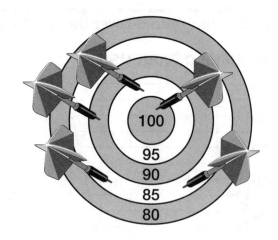

Solve.

1. Gina has 3 cats that weigh 12 pounds, 15 pounds, and 18 pounds. What is the range of their weights?

2. What is the mean weight of Gina's cats?

3. Dean earns $9.70 an hour. Sabrina earns $8.25. Luigi earns $8.51. What is their mean hourly pay?

4. What is the median hourly pay for Dean, Sabrina, and Luigi?

5. On a fishing trip, 5 sharks were caught. They weighed 230, 528, 309, 247, and 216 pounds. What is the range of weights?

6. What is the mean weight of a shark caught on the trip?

7. What is the median weight of a shark caught on the trip?

8. The populations of 3 neighboring towns are 6,400; 3,768; and 5,561. What is the mean population?

A **circle graph** is used to show parts of a whole.

Use these circle graphs to answer the questions and solve each problem.

**ONE MUSICIAN'S
SOURCES OF INCOME**

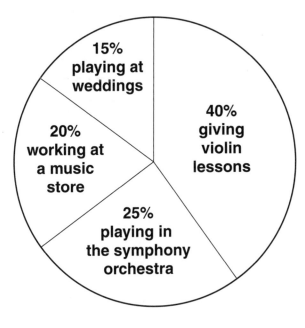

1. What does this circle graph show?

   _____

   _____

2. What percent of income does the musician earn from the symphony? _____

3. What is the biggest source of income?

   _____

4. Does the musician earn more playing in the symphony or working at a music store?

   _____

5. Which activity provides the least income?

   _____

_____

6. What does this circle graph show?

   _____

   _____

7. What kind of instrument makes up the largest part of the orchestra?

   _____

8. What percent of the orchestra do brass instruments make up? _____

9. Are there more percussion or woodwind instruments? _____

10. What percent is woodwinds? _____

11. What fraction is that? _____

12. If there are 100 instruments in the orchestra, how many are string instruments? _____

**INSTRUMENTS IN A
SYMPHONY ORCHESTRA**

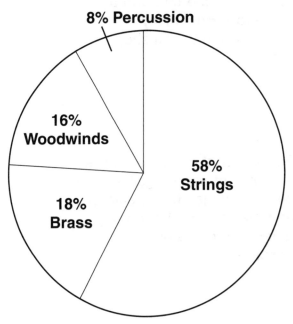

Some problems can be solved by making a tree diagram.

Camp T-shirts are available in 4 colors: red, green, yellow, and blue. The printing on them can be either black or white. How many different combinations are possible?

The tree diagram shows that there are 8 different combinations.

T-shirt	Printing	Combination
red	white	red/white
	black	red/black
green	white	green/white
	black	green/black
yellow	white	yellow/white
	black	yellow/black
blue	white	blue/white
	black	blue/black

Make a tree diagram to solve each problem.

1. Perry is planning his day at camp. He can hike or ride in the morning. He can swim or canoe in the afternoon. How many different ways can he spend the day?

2. Aurora brought white shorts, red shorts, and blue shorts to camp. She also brought a red top, a blue top, and a white top. How many different outfits can she make?

3. For dinner, the campers have a choice of hamburger or chicken, vegetable or salad, and pie or cake. How many different dinners are possible?

Probability is the chance of something happening.

The chance of randomly choosing the striped marble from this group is 1 out of 5. Probability can also be written as a fraction:

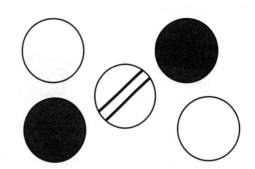

$$\frac{1}{5} \begin{array}{l} \leftarrow \text{number of favorable} \\ \text{outcomes (striped marbles)} \\ \leftarrow \text{number of possible} \\ \text{outcomes (marbles)} \end{array}$$

Write a fraction for each probability.

What is the probability of the spinner landing on—	What is the probability of randomly picking—	What is the probability of randomly picking—

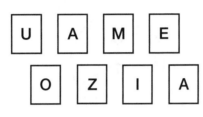

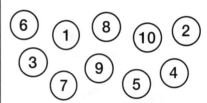

1. black?

2. white?

3. gray?

4. the letter A?

5. the letter M?

6. a consonant?

7. a vowel?

8. the number 1?

9. a two-digit number?

10. an even number?

11. a multiple of 2?

Solve.

12. Hatsu tosses a penny. What is the probability that it will land tails up?

13. Emma has 4 red bows, 3 blue ones, and 2 green ones. If she picks one without looking, what is the probability that it will be green?

14. There are 3 blue pens, 2 black ones, and 1 red one. What is the probability of randomly picking a blue pen?

15. A box contains 12 chocolates that look the same. However, 5 are creams, 4 are caramels, and 3 are nuts. What is the probability of randomly picking a cream?

Sometimes probability is a fraction equal to 1 or to 0.

The probability of choosing a black marble from this group is 1, or **certain**.

$$\frac{5}{5} = 1$$

The probability of choosing a white marble from this group is 0, or **impossible**.

$$\frac{0}{5} = 0$$

Write each probability.

What is the probability of randomly picking—

1. a circle?

2. a triangle?

3. a star?

4. a shape?

What is the probability of the spinner landing on—

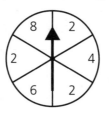

5. the number 2?

6. the number 4?

7. an even number?

8. an odd number?

What is the probability of randomly picking—

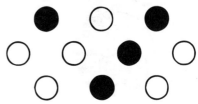

9. a black ball?

10. a white ball?

11. a black or a white ball?

12. a striped ball?

Solve.

13. Sean has 3 sweaters. All of them are red. If he picks one at random, what is the probability that the sweater will be blue?

14. A box holds 12 chocolate cupcakes. If Judy takes one at random, what is the probability that it will be chocolate?

15. Felicia has 12 books. There are 6 mysteries and the rest are science fiction. If she picks one at random, what is the probability that it will be a mystery?

16. Darrell has 3 $1 bills and 1 $5 bill in his wallet. If he takes a bill out without looking, what is the probability that it will be a $10 bill?